At All Times

Devotionals for Praise and Worship to
Empower You for Daily Living

Donna Renay Patrick

WestBow
P R E S S
A DIVISION OF THOMAS NELSON

WestBow Press books may be ordered through booksellers or by contacting:

WestBow Press
A Division of Thomas Nelson
1663 Liberty Drive
Bloomington, IN 47403
www.westbowpress.com
1-(866) 928-1240

Because of the dynamic nature of the Internet, any web addresses or links contained in this book may have changed since publication and may no longer be valid. The views expressed in this work are solely those of the author and do not necessarily reflect the views of the publisher, and the publisher hereby disclaims any responsibility for them.

Any people depicted in stock imagery provided by Thinkstock are models, and such images are being used for illustrative purposes only.

Certain stock imagery © Thinkstock.

ISBN: 978-1-4497-4368-0 (sc)
ISBN: 978-1-4497-4367-3 (hc)
ISBN: 978-1-4497-4369-7 (e)

Library of Congress Control Number: 2012905139

Printed in the United States of America

WestBow Press rev. date: 5/07/2012

Dedication

To my Lord and Savior, Jesus Christ, and to my mother, Mrs. Louise Patrick, who saw to it that I developed a relationship with Him.

To my sister Debra, who went to be with the Lord during production of this work. I know how proud you would have been to see this book come to fruition. Thanks for always loving me and being my sister.

To my niece Jackye, for being the niece I've always wanted. I love being your "Auntiee."

Posthumously, to my sister, Jackye, and my father, Grandee Patrick. I thank the Lord for every moment He gave us to be a family. I miss you terribly.

None of us get through life all alone. Not a single one of us made it to where we are without help. There have been so many people in my lifetime who have prayed for me, nurtured, and helped to shape me into the woman of God I have become. Some are yet alive; others are now in the eternal presence of God. This work is also dedicated to you.

I want to acknowledge my Pastor, leaders, Music Ministry, and the entire Christian Chapel Temple of Faith C.M.E. Church family for their prayers, love, support, their commitment to next level prayer and worship, and for being God's incubator as I have grown and developed in praise and worship ministry.

Contents

Foreword

It was a moment of spiritual hunger those precious segments of our lives when we realized that God can speak to us in special ways. I recognized while reading a descriptive reflection of worship that this writer had a real connection with the subject. Further encounters revealed a gifted musician and writer who transcends the often one-dimensional focus of what many attempt to describe as worship. Instead I found a writer inspired to draw from the wellsprings of experience and biblical truths and offer a realistic and factual approach to worship and praise. I am describing one who identifies with the passion of praise and the awesome splendor of having been in the presence of the One Whom we worship. Ms. Donna Patrick, who has been gifted with a rare sense of practical relatedness in teaching and writing, offers all of us a helpful guide to enrich our spiritual lives. Ms. Patrick is not only academically prepared but also spiritually enlightened to dig deep into the realms of the basic requirements of worship and praise. She unfolds the thoughtful insights of our joys and sorrows and leads us to the victorious realm that worship can carry us. Ms. Patrick's unique grasp of the true essence of musical inter-relatedness to praise and the worship experience is refreshing. This book is a true guide to ease us in moments of despair and discover hope in our ability to be free in the spirit. Please share the joys of the power of the Lord generated by this tremendous writer, musician and teacher.

Gratefully,
Your Pastor and Friend,
Jerome McNeil, Jr., Ph.D.
Christian Chapel CME Temple of Faith
Chief Spiritual Officer

Preface

My mother spoke a book into my life some years ago. When I first entered the ministry of praise & worship, my mom said something about "that book you're going to write." I thought nothing of it at the time, but then God began to orchestrate some things surrounding this ministry He called me into, and a "book" began to take shape. Then he placed me among a congregation of people who only added to what mom had told me a long time ago. So when I began to get serious about putting this book together, the Lord began dealing with me.

This book is one born out of periods of brokenness, pain, victory, frustration, hope, weariness, waiting, tears, and very often, sacrificial praise. If you give God a chance He will show you that He will turn your pain into a praise. He will use your brokenness to elevate you to a new level of greatness for Him. The devotionals you are about to read address many different areas of the Christian experience. I grew up in the Antioch Missionary Baptist Church of Decatur, Illinois, where people "joined church" on their "Christian experience." I did not understand what that meant; I still don't. But Christian experience to me, means "your experience as a Christian;" your personal experience walking with the Lord and what He has taught you as you have remained in relationship with Him. That is exactly what these devotionals (some may call them "meditations" or "inspirations") are about. I am sharing with you what God has shared with me in my Christian experience, and specifically, as it relates to my ministry in the areas of praise and worship.

Introduction

Praise and worship are two subjects that are often confusing to some. Many in the church don't know where to start to learn more about these two extensive topics. The best source is, of course, the Word of God. Too often, we look to music to define our attitudes about praise and worship. The truth is neither of them totally encompass the other. Coming together on Sunday morning to sing great songs from a great choir, with great musicians at the helm does not necessarily mean we worshiped. Music must not be the measuring rod to whether or not we've worshiped. Music is one thing – worship is quite another.

This book has been written to elevate our understanding of the power that praise and worship bring to our lives as Christian believers. My prayer is that the reader will wrap his or her life around the scripture passages found with these devotionals, meditate on them, and go about your day with an attitude of praise and a heart filled with the worship of God. Many areas of the Christian experience are addressed through each devotional. Each has been written as a short, easy to digest daily meditation with scripture references for personal reflection. They are intended to be practical and fit for everyday life application. My prayer is that these devotionals strengthen your personal commitment to make praise and worship a daily part of your life. I pray that you are blessed and encouraged by them.

To the true and living God I worship,
Donna R. Patrick

Where Is Your Secret Place?

He that **dwelleth** in the secret place of the
Most High shall abide under the shadow of the
Almighty. I will **say** of the Lord, He **is** my **refuge**
and my **fortress:** my God; **in him** will I trust.
(Psalm 91:1,2) (KJV) (emphasis mine)

I do not know about you, but if God, through the pages of His
Word, is inviting me to abide (stay, live, hang out, be there awhile,
spend some time) under His shadow, guess what? He doesn't have
to tell me twice. If being under His shadow means I have peace,
deliverance, solutions to my problems, strength for the journey, and
power to walk in my calling, then the best place for you and I to be
is under His shadow. All we have to do is dwell in His secret place.
Notice it says he that *dwelleth;* it does not say, "He that stops by every
now and then." This Psalm is **so** powerful! As you read further you
will see what God will do for those who make their home in Him.

What does it mean to "dwell in His secret place"? When you
have had a good day, thank Him. When you have had a bad day,
run to Him. Ask Him to lead you day by day, moment by moment.
Determine you are going to walk under His authority in every area
of your life. That is dwelling in His secret place. Spend time in prayer
and praise; allow His Word to permeate your heart. Instead of just
getting in the Word, let the Word **get in you.** That is how we dwell
in His secret place.

Praise Him for being your hiding place (refuge) and your
protection (fortress). Then worship Him for being the Most High
God.

Is Praise What YOU Do?

for the battle is not yours, but God's. And when they
began singing and praising, the Lord set ambushes against
the sons of Ammon, Moab, and Mount Seir, who had
come against Judah.
(2 Chronicles 20:15, 22) (NASB)

There is a very popular song on the gospel music scene recorded by Shekinah Glory Ministries entitled "Praise Is What I Do." A portion of the lyrics say: "Praise is what I do when I wanna be close to You. . ." This song goes on to say "I vow to praise You through the good and the bad." . . ."whether happy or sad." It is easy to praise God when things are going well. But what about when things are *not* going well in our own eyes? What if trouble meets you at the door when you get to work this morning? What if God totally changes your plans for the day? Will you still praise Him; even if for a moment? Somebody might need to spend the day just praising Him inside of your heart. God hears even a whisper of praise, as long as it is coming out of a sincere, yielded heart. Whatever is on your agenda today, make it a priority to lavish some praise on the God Who gave you another today. He is Lord of the day, and He is listening for your praise.

Fear Factor

*. . .**Fear not***: for I have redeemed thee, I have called [thee]
by name; thou [art] mine;
(Isaiah 43:1) (emphasis mine)

What are you afraid of? If we're all honest, there is something or someone that strikes some level of fear in us. It may not be a paralyzing fear, or anything that completely immobilizes us; but it may be something that at the very least produces some level of anxiety, to the point that we are taken aback for a moment. First, let's consider two types of fear: human fear and reverential fear. On the human side, some of the things that may produce anxiety in us might be the fear of water, or heights. Some may fear snakes or certain animals, or flying. We live in an uncertain economy; some of us may fear losing a job, or losing hard-earned retirement monies, or our homes. All of these things can make us uncomfortable so we tend to shy away from them at all costs. But what about reverential fear? How do the words "reverential" and "fear" even show up in the same sentence?

Reverential fear points to the fear of God. The Word of God is very clear that He is a God to be feared (Psalm 96:4). This is the kind of fear that drives us to worship God. The Word also says that He is a gracious and merciful God (Psalm 86:15). When we reverence God we respect His highness, His holiness, and His majesty. When we have embraced a reverential fear of God, we have ordered our steps in His direction, patterned our lives after His standard and make decisions based on who we know Him to be. When we fear God there are just certain things that, if the Holy Spirit is alive on the inside of us, we just will not do.

But now that we have established the difference, let's look at what else the Word says about fear. First of all Paul tells us in II Timothy 1:7 that fear (of man) is not of God. In other words, God **did not** give us a spirit of fear. This word spirit has many Biblical uses, but for purposes of this devotional the meaning we want is "the power by which the human being feels, thinks, and decides." So when we talk about having a "spirit of fear" we are talking about that part of our human makeup the enables us to feel, think, and decide (or the power of choice). So we can choose to be fearful, or we can choose to walk in soundness of mind. According to scripture, in place of fear God has given us power, love, and a sound mind. If the Word says it is right NOT to fear, then it must be wrong TO fear.

Whatever you're afraid of how do you let go of it? First, recognize that God is God and He will be praised and worshiped (Psalm 150:2). Second, **surrender** your fear(s) to Him in private and public worship. Third, learn to see Him as a loving Father who cares about you, and accept His love. Part of accepting His love for you is bowing low before Him in worship. True worship of God in spirit and in truth (John 4:23-24) will bring transformation to the fearful heart. A **renewed** mind in the Word is a mind NOT set on fear!

Consider these passages to help you let go of human fear and embrace reverential fear:

Isaiah 41:10: ***Fear thou not****; for I am with thee; be not dismayed; for I am thy God: I will strengthen thee. . .*

Psalm 27:1: *The Lord is my light and my salvation;* ***whom shall I fear?***

Psalm 34:4: *I sought the Lord, and he heard me, and **delivered me from all my fears;***

Psalm 34:7; *The angel of the Lord **encampeth round about them that fear him***, *and delivereth them;*

Psalm 34:9: *O **fear the Lord, ye his saints: for there is no want to them that fear him.***

Favor, Not Fear

For surely, O LORD, you bless the righteous; you
surround them with your favor as with a shield.
(Psalm 5:12) (NIV) (emphasis mine)

When you try to fuse favor and fear together, you will find that they are like oil and water - they don't play well together. It pays to know who you are in Christ; and what the Word of God says about us as children of the King. When we know who we are in Christ the enemy cannot play havoc with us. Satan is the father of lies (John 8:44), but when we know who we are according to the Word of God, the lies and tricks of the enemy will not take root in our spirit because we have too much of the Word on the inside of us. We have to know as saints that God has already given us favor. However, it is up to us to **operate** in it. Too often we allow fear to take root and, again, we have to know what the Word says about us. The Word says that fear is not of God (2 Tim. 1:7). We can surround ourselves with fear, but God surrounds us with His favor. Jesus invested too much in us at the cross of Calvary for us to remain down, depressed, dejected, or afflicted in any area of our lives. God's Word says we are *surrounded* by His favor. When you run a check on the word "favor" you will find such descriptive terms as "pleasure," "delight," "goodwill," and "acceptance." Go ahead and apply for that job you don't think you are qualified for. Go ahead and search for your first house. Go ahead and start that business. If you know your vision is from God, then move forward in it as you stand on the Word of God. God has given us favor; He has **not** endowed us with fear. I choose to believe all that God's Word says about me. Will you believe it for your life? Will you stand in the face of fear or rejection and say, "I am surrounded by God's favor"?

Clean Your Gun

Now the Lord said to Joshua, "Do not fear or be
dismayed. Take all the people of war with you and arise,
go up to Ai;. . ."
(Joshua 8:1) (NASB)

I have a friend who retired from the United States Army having
earned the rank of Major. I learned from him how important it
is for soldiers to be acutely familiar with their weapons. Soldiers
are not prepared for battle unless they know how, and when to
use their weapons. Soldiers also have to know how to care for their
weapons and keep them in good working order. When we engage
in true, heartfelt praise to God, it is a weapon against the enemy
overtaking us in times of attack. The praises of God can also lead
to our deliverance. King Jehoshaphat used the praises of God as the
nation of Judah headed to the battleground. A very important fact
of military training is that soldiers know and be trained on how his/
her weapon operates; and how and when to use it. As soldiers in the
spirit realm, we train our tongues and our inner man as we speak
forth the praises of God *daily*—not just on Sunday. Enemy attack
is a good training ground for firing our weapons of praise. However,
don't wait until the enemy shows himself to speak out God's praise.
Be ready at any moment to use your weapon. That takes getting into
the Word and training your spirit to know the power that **belongs** to
you as you shout unto God (Psalm 47:1). One thing you **cannot** do
with your mouth closed is shout! Living the praise lifestyle doesn't
mean problems won't come to you. It does mean, however, that with
the high praises of God on your lips, no adversity can overtake you
because you have trained your spirit to continually bless God. Paul

and Silas were physically in jail, but spiritually they were free. That's how they were able to sing in that dark, lonely jail cell. They knew how to use their weapons in the form of prayer and song. They kept their guns cleaned and oiled-—ready to use.

Clean Your Gun, Part 2

Now the Lord said to Joshua, "Do not fear or be
dismayed. *Take all the people of war with you* and arise,
go up to Ai;. . ."
(Joshua 8:1) (emphasis mine)

In the previous devotional of this same title the focus was on
praise as a weapon, and how we should keep our weapon clean,
in good working order, and always knowing how to use it. King
Jehoshaphat used the praises of God as the nation of Judah headed
to the battleground. In today's meditation, Joshua is preparing for
battle with the small city of Ai. There is much more to the story,
but for purposes of this meditation, God told Joshua to take the
people of war with him. Who do you have who can go to war with
you when things get rough? Who is in your camp who can help you
praise your way out of your circumstances? Those who know how to
fight the enemy with their praise live above their circumstances. Are
there believers in your life who use their Bibles to train for battle,
rather than for just looking sanctimonious on Sunday morning?
Believers in Jesus Christ know that intentional prayer, praise, and
worship to God is their life blood; they understand them to be
weapons of war - weapons of breakthrough! (Psalm 107:15-16 NIV).
In the spirit realm people of war are really people of the Word! They
know how to take the sword of the Spirit (Eph. 6:17) and use it
against our enemy, the devil. Take personal inventory for a minute.
Are you a person of war?

Is Unity Missing?

Only conduct yourselves in a manner worthy of the gospel
of Christ, so that whether I come and see you or remain
absent, I will hear of you that you are **standing firm in
one spirit,** with one [a] mind **striving together** for the
faith of the gospel;
(Phil. 1:27) (NASB) (emphasis mine)

As believers in Jesus Christ are we walking together, working together, holding one another up, and loving God together? How do we treat one another? Do we attend church each Sunday, and perhaps during the week for various ministry meetings or services, only to leave the same way we came? Does the spiritual food we receive never infiltrate our entire being? Toward the end of Acts Chapter 2 we see language such as "had all things in common," and "with one accord." Is unity missing in your private or public worship experience? Is it missing in your ministry? Our relationships with other people are directly tied to our relationship with God. The horizontal (how we relate to people) affects the vertical (how we relate to God), and the vertical affects the horizontal. God is concerned about how we treat one another in the Body of Christ. We should be concerned also. Does the enemy have a stranglehold on our congregations so that division dwells among us? Think about that.

Face Down the Enemy

*. . . the accuser of our brethren has been thrown down,
he who accuses them before our God day and night. And
they overcame him because of the blood of the Lamb and
because of the word of their testimony. . .*
(Rev. 12:10-11) (NASB)

Every Christian, regardless of denomination encounters enemy activity in some area of his or her life. Regardless of how long we have walked with the Lord, our enemy, the devil, constantly stands against any facet of God's spiritual authority. When I did some research into the word "enemy" I found out there are at least four different uses of it in scripture; but the common denominator seemed to be opposition. From beginning to end, the Word of God makes references to those who faced opposition from the devil himself or from people who stood in opposition to God's vessel.

We just concluded a revival at my church that focused specifically on the family, and the different ways the devil will attack the family unit. The speaker did not leave though, without telling us how to stand, or face down, the enemy of our marriages and families. He talked about binding and loosing, and calling demonic spirits by name according to where they have chosen to operate. How do you face down the enemy attacking your finances, your marriage, your job, the relationship you have with your children, your ministry, and a host of other human endeavors? When the enemy boldly tempted Jesus in the wilderness, Jesus just as boldly faced him down with the Word of God. The prophet Elijah found himself facing down the enemy in the person of Jezebel. Elijah remained true to the mission God had assigned to him and kept prophesying. When

Nehemiah went back to rebuild the wall at Jerusalem, he faced very real and intentional opposition; but he kept working - sometimes with a weapon in one hand and a tool in the other. King Jehoshaphat faced down the enemy with prayer and praise. He and all of Judah praised God *on the way* to the battle ground. As they did so, God set ambushments against their enemies, who all rose up against and destroyed one another.

Are you facing the devil himself or a person (or situation) operating in conjunction with him? I hope our reference text above will guide you. Begin to stand up in your authority as a child of God and plead the blood of Jesus. Then line up your words with scripture. God already knows what you're facing. Begin to tell your battle about God, and His ability to bring you out of your dilemma. Face down the enemy with praise and worship. Don't just think it, speak it! The enemy cannot read your thoughts, but he can hear what you say! I challenge every reader to call out the enemy. God has given you authority (Luke 10:19); you hold the keys to your deliverance.

Survive Your Brokenness with Worship

*. . .and he came into the house of the Lord
and worshiped. (2 Sam 12:20) (NASB)*

On the surface, brokenness is not a good thing. But a closer look can lead you to God. Brokenness can take on many forms, but the feeling is just about the same. Sometimes we have to be broken from being impatient; some of us need to be broken of self-pride; others must learn to love others. I believe God uses our brokenness to bring us closer to Him, and bring us back into His presence. We are always in His abiding presence because He is omnipresent, but it is His manifest presence that I'm referring to. Brokenness has a cleansing property to it; in other words God can use our brokenness to see what is really on the inside of us – what is really in our hearts. In our brokenness God examines the purity of our motives. If we handle our brokenness the right way, it can lead to power.

David was a broken man when the child conceived in an adulterous relationship lay dying. After the child died David worshiped God. Hannah's heart broke every time Peninnah taunted her because she had not yet conceived a child. But when God did open Hannah's womb and give her a son who would become a prophet of Israel, she praised God (I Sam 2:1-2). Job was left with his life, and a wife whose remedy for her husband's pain was "curse God and die," but he still blessed God (Job 1:21).

If you are going through a period of brokenness of whatever nature, maybe God is trying to tell you something. Perhaps He has a word to get across to you in this experience. You will survive this season of brokenness through your worship. Yes, you're in pain; yes, you have questions that seem to have no answers; okay, you feel helpless. But there *is* something you can do - get in God's face in worship. Let God know that you know He is still God and that He loves you. Love on Him, spend time with, talk to, and bless Him. There is a way out. The sooner you get into God's presence in true, heart-felt, Holy Spirit-controlled worship, the sooner you will see things a little clearer from God's perspective.

God Has You Covered

*As the mountains are round about Jerusalem, so the Lord
is round about his people from henceforth even for ever.
(Psalm 125:2) (KJV)*

I heard a local pastor's broadcast this morning, and he said something
I thought was profound. He said "If the devil can't shut you up, he'll
attempt to shut you down." Now, for me that was a whole day's worth
of encouragement. I could have turned him off at that point because
that was a rich word! But I kept listening, and as I did, the Holy
Spirit began talking to me. What did Daniel, Elijah, and Peter have
in common? Yes, they were all very bold servants of almighty God.
But they shared another very interesting characteristic: they all refused
to allow the enemy to shut them down. Daniel's enemies conspired
against him because he wouldn't stop praying three times a day - it
landed him in a den of lions. When Elijah killed the prophets of Baal,
Jezebel wanted Elijah dead. By Herod's order Peter landed on death
row for preaching Jesus. Daniel kept praying, Elijah kept prophesying,
and Peter kept preaching. They were all candidates for, and recipients
of, God's deliverance. The enemy couldn't shut them up, so he tried
to shut them down. Well, the enemy's tactics have not changed much
over thousands of years; he still attempts to shut down your ministry,
your effectiveness, your witness, your mission, your vision, and your
God-given dream. But I want to encourage somebody. Just as God
surrounded Daniel, Elijah, and Peter, He is surrounding you with
His favor (*Also see* Psalm 125:1-2). When we walk close to God He is
keeping us under His divine protection so that whatever direction we
turn He is there. Keep moving boldly into what God has called you
to do. Praise God because He has you covered.

Praise and Affliction

Many are the afflictions of the righteous; **but the Lord**
delithvereth him out of them all.
(Psalm 34:19) (KJV) (Emphasis mine)

In our title you may wonder why I would couple these two terms together. "Praise" and "thanksgiving" coupled together makes sense. "Praise" and "worship" go well together, as we all know. Even "praise" and "rejoicing" are a logical set. But "praise" and "affliction"? *Affliction* can be defined as *any situation or circumstance that produces suffering or pain,* whether physical or otherwise. As Isaiah prophesied Jesus' suffering in Chapter 53 of his book (v4), we read that Jesus was "smitten of God and afflicted." But in the very next verse it says "and with His stripes we are healed." Paul tells us in Ephesians 2:13 that we are brought near to God through Jesus' shed blood. Ephesians Chapter 1 speaks clearly of our adoption, inheritance, redemption, and forgiveness all because of Jesus' affliction. Romans 8:17 teaches us we are heirs with God and joint heirs with Christ. Jesus' affliction produced for us salvation, heirship, anointing, healing and many other rights that I don't have space to cover in this devotional. So just maybe there is something about our own personal affliction that we ought not run from. We don't like affliction in whatever form because it's painful. No matter how big your Bible is, suffering and pain are a part of our Christian experience, along with the joys and victories. But while we may not praise Him **for** the affliction, we can praise Him **in** it. Remember the Word says, *"Many. . .but the Lord. . ."*

Seeking God's Face On My Face

And all the angels were standing around the throne
and around the elders and the four living creatures;
and they fell on their faces before the throne and
worshiped God, saying, "Amen, blessing and glory
and wisdom and thanksgiving and honor and power
and might, be to our God forever and ever. Amen."
(Revelation 7:11-12), (NASB)

One of the things that true worship demands is humble submission. There is just no way around it. God wants every part of us, even with our issues. We don't have to hesitate to bring our issues to God; He can handle them. Remember He is our Creator and He already knows the things we struggle with.

His Word tells us to constantly seek His face. We seek His face in prayer, and through the reading and study of His Word. But I want to offer another useful tool to seek the face of God, and that is seek Him on our faces; literally bow low - as low as we can go with our faces to the floor. Talk about humble submission! We can physically go no lower before God than on our faces. But don't just stop at a bowed body; be certain your heart is bowed also. It isn't about merely the bodily position we are taking because worship is always a matter of the heart. As much fighting and resisting that we sometimes do, all of that has to come to an end on our faces. On our faces we are flat, stretched out, not looking up or around, just looking down; only our hearts are looking up to God. The inhabitants of heaven got on their faces to worship God; they humbled themselves and they were already in the eternal presence of God.

We have not yet entered eternity because we are yet on this side of time, but be challenged in your spirit that if God has you in "wait" mode, begin to wait on your face. If God's promises to you seem delayed get on your face. If your spiritual walk seems stagnant, get on your face and allow God to minister to your spirit. Talk to Him and worship Him on your face. Somehow when we are on our faces before a high, holy God, He comes a little closer.

Courage to Praise, Courage to Worship

I will bless the Lord at all times. . .
(Psalm 34:1(a)) (NASB)

Truly, it takes courage to praise God at all times as the psalmist declares. Based on some of the events of David's life he had plenty of reason to silence his praise IF that's what he chose to do. But David was a praiser; he was a worshiper. So when David went through his personal struggles he mustered up the courage to praise God in spite of his current condition. As I write this meditation I am thinking of situations where it was dark in my life and all I had to hold on to was my faith. God's Word was the only light I had (Psalm 119:105).

I want to encourage somebody to praise God until your fear subsides. Search the Word of God to learn who He is, and who you are in Him so you can worship Him with the proper perspective. Put hedonism behind you and understand that worship really isn't about us and what we want; it's all about Him. Fight the temptation to be a spectator in the worship experience and come to God with a repentant heart. God doesn't want any of us holding on to the guilt of our past; He has a much deeper plan. Your freedom lies only in Him. Trust Him to free you from every hindrance that may be blocking your view of Him in true worship and praise.

God told Joshua to be strong and courageous (Joshua 1:9); just as we must be in order to lay aside those things that stop us from worshiping God the way He so desires. Your trust and your courage must lie in Him.

The Wounded Worshiper

> So David arose from the ground, washed, anointed
> himself, and changed his clothes; and he came into the
> house of the Lord and worshiped.
> (II Samuel 12:20(a)) (NASB)

King David loved the Lord with all of his heart. But he messed up. When David sinned with Bathsheba it may seem for a moment that He had no conscience; but when the child born from his sin died, David was deeply wounded. No one around him could console him. He was a broken man with a secret; the secret was he knew where to go for healing.

How many of us are walking around with a wounded heart or spirit, and your personal worship of God is suffering because of it? If your private worship is suffering, you are probably not enjoying the corporate worship experience to the fullest either. You're not free to encounter God's presence the way you would like because of something you should have let go of a long time ago. God is a God of freedom and he wants you to be free so you can worship Him in spirit *and* in truth. What holds true in the human realm is also true in the spirit realm: even the strongest, most skillful soldiers sometimes get wounded in the battle. Take your wounds to God, whatever they are, and let Him perform spiritual surgery. You do not have to keep hurting.

What's Hindering You?

Wherefore seeing we also are compassed about with so
great a cloud of witnesses, let us lay aside every weight,
and the sin which doth so easily beset us, and let us run
with patience the race that is set before us.
(Hebrews 12:1) (KJV)

You have seen devotionals from me that deal specifically with
the varying reasons we **do** (or should) praise and worship God,
but I thought it fitting to share a series of meditations about why
we **don't**.

In his lifetime, Bro. Glenn Burleigh shared with the world all
of the divinely-inspired musical genius that God would allow while
he lived with us on earth. One of the products of that genius was a
song he composed entitled, "Lay Aside Every Weight," based upon
today's passage, and others. A portion of the lyrics of that song went
like this: "whatever it is that's keeping you from serving Jesus put it
off. . .". What is keeping you from serving Jesus in continuous praise
and intentional worship? Countless people sit in church Sunday after
Sunday and miss worship for a variety of reasons. I don't want you
to be one of them.

God has never *requested* praise or worship from us; He has
always *commanded* both. Yes, God is a God of freedom; He loves us
in freedom, and He leaves us free to choose whether to love Him in
return. He bestows on us the freedom to choose whether to serve
Him in daily, intentional praise and worship. We are going to look
at the various reasons believers miss worship on Sunday, and why
we may not engage in praise or worship on a daily basis. Some of us
may not even realize that the things we carry within us are hindering

our praise, and stifling our worship. But I hope during this series of coming devotionals, through the power of the Holy Spirit, that I will perhaps bowl down your alley, offering you the freedom to lay aside whatever is hindering you from praising and worshiping God the way He intended.

Is Guilt Holding You Back?

*. . .lay aside every weight, and the sin which doth so easily
beset us. . .*
(Hebrews 12:1) (KJV)

Moving on with our series dealing with those things that hinder our worship to God, let's look at guilt. Some people find it hard to worship because they are guilty about something. They love the Lord, but they messed up and the enemy won't let them forget it. The "enemy" may take the form of the person who saw them mess up; or that old friend who says to them, "I knew you when. . ." and has not accepted the change Christ has made in this person's life. Guilt can feel like it weighs a ton. It can rob a person of the freedom God gives us in praise and in worship. Sometimes church folk won't let you forget.

True worship in spirit and in truth, be it public or private, takes the focus off of you, and rightly places it on God. God is ready to take your guilt, but you must loosen your grip on it. He wants you to be free of it, but you must surrender all the maintenance and upkeep you've done on it. God does not want you to carry all of that, and you don't have to anymore. Don't you want to be free? Don't you want to serve God in worship with nothing holding you back? Recognize that guilt is an enemy to the worshiper, and turn your back on it. Jesus has already dealt with your guilt at the cross of Calvary. Receive Him and receive your freedom.

Hedonism as a Hindrance to Worship

For great is the Lord, and greatly to be praised; He is to be
feared above all gods.
(Psalm 96:4) (NASB)

Hedonism has to be high on the list of things that keep us from
experiencing God's presence in true worship. There are different
schools of thought on the meaning and interpretation of the term
hedonism. But the one to be addressed here is the theory that people are
motivated only by what they want, their own happiness, and their self-
interests. That works for awhile in a chosen profession, in school, where
to go on vacation, what kinds of books to read, what movies to see, or
even what church we choose to attend. But it will never work when it
comes to in spirit and in truth worship (John 4:23-24).

True, heartfelt, God-focused worship is not contingent upon
good feelings, one's own happiness, or self-interest. The kind of
worship God desires is based wholly on surrender - a total surrender
that says, "God, all I want is You." All too often in our churches
performance is the norm, rather than the manifest presence of God.
Music is played that makes people "feel" good; eloquent prayers are
offered, and sermons are spoken absent the power of God because
it is ourselves we are trying to please, rather than God. Am I saying
God doesn't want us to live as happy, fulfilled people? No, of course
not. What I am saying is that God never intended for us to place
our own personal happiness above Him. Worship is not about
what we want; it is about what God wants. He desires to receive
the glory in every aspect of our lives. Unfortunately in many of our
churches today worship is a business. For some, church is a business.
But worship is not mere business to God - it is very *personal* to Him

because worship that flows out of a sincere heart touches the very heart of God. Worship that moves God flows from the heart that has been in touch with God all week long; and out of a spirit fortified by the presence of the Holy Spirit.

Worship really isn't about us - it's about God.

Spectatorism in the Worship Experience

> you also, as living stones. . .offer up spiritual sacrifices
> acceptable to God through Jesus Christ. But you are a
> chosen race, a royal priesthood, a holy nation, a people
> for God's own possession, that you may proclaim the
> excellencies of him who has called you out of darkness
> into His marvelous light;
> (I Peter 2:5, 9) (NASB)

One more hindrance that is sometimes present in the corporate worship experience that deserves a closer look is that of spectatorism - just coming to church to see what's happening. God has created each one of us, no matter where you've come from, no matter what you've done, to be a worshiper of Him. If you have been a *watcher* rather than a *participant* in the worship experience, I hope, in the power of the Holy Spirit, to change your current perspective.

It's easy to do. Being a musician myself, I can certainly admit that at times there is so much activity going on with the worship leader, the team, the band, or the choir, that if we're not careful, we'll miss God in all of the music. That is not our intention, but it happens. But no matter how great the music is flowing, our ultimate destination is the manifest presence of God. God has made us all a kingdom of priests unto Himself. The most we can do to honor God is to fill our hearts with more of Him, so that in the Sunday morning worship experience we can't help but give to Him out of a prepared, surrendered heart. Worship is never about what we can get from God, but what we can give to Him; and what he wants from us is - well, **all** of us. He wants our hearts, our minds, and our bodies. We are His, and He deserves for us to give back to Him what is already His. Whether your role is preacher or layperson, active or inactive in a ministry, being a worshiper is a role that God desires each of us to fulfill.

Unconfessed Sin as a Hindrance

If I regard iniquity in my heart The Lord will not hear me.
(Psalm 66:18) (KJV)

The sixty-sixth number of Psalms holds so much for us; there is praise, exaltation, testimony, and invitation. Verse seven holds a warning for the rebellious. But in all of that the writer of this particular Psalm makes a profound acknowledgement. The writer makes it personal saying, "If I regard iniquity in my heart God will not hear me." How many times have churchgoers attempted to come into God's holy presence in the corporate or the private worship experience knowing we had not come clean before Him? We knew there were things in our hearts that did not belong there; or there may have been something that had contaminated our spirit, yet we made the attempt to worship anyway? Where was our worship at that point?

Worship is two-way communication - it is us talking to God, and allowing God to talk to us. But in order to make that two-way communication happen we have a responsibility as believers and as worshipers. When we choose to worship God in the manner He intended according to John 4:23-24, there must be confession. Is it possible to truly worship Him in spirit and in truth while harboring unconfessed sin in our lives? Just as every believer is included in Romans 3:23, likewise every believer is included in First John 1:9. Just as all have sinned, all have an opportunity to confess our sins and experience God's forgiveness.

My prayer is that every believer in Jesus Christ - whether in church or out - will search his or her own heart for unconfessed sin that may be hindering the liberating worship experience that Jesus died and rose to give us. Don't just confess it, but honestly confront yourself with it. Release it to God, and turn your back on whatever was blocking your true worship.

An Improper View of God

. . .and the Lord swept the sea back by a strong east wind
all night, and turned the sea into dry land. . .; And the
waters returned. . . Thus the Lord saved Israel that day
from the hand of the Egyptians. . .
(Exodus 14: 21, 28, 30) (NASB)

If it is not unconfessed sin that is keeping you from worshiping
God, then perhaps it is because you have an improper perspective
of Him. All throughout scripture, from Genesis to Revelation God
is letting us know Who He is. Though He is a God of judgment,
He is also a God of justice. Yes, He deals with the disobedient, but
He also loves and uplifts those who choose to trust Him and enjoy
relationship with Him. Yes, He judged Eli's entire house because of
his sons' disobedience. But He also, in spite of David's sin, established
his throne forever, telling David as long as his sons obeyed God the
house of David would never lack a man on the throne of Israel.

Many people view God as a tyrant who is much too angry with
them to ever receive their heartfelt worship. But God has commanded
worship; the only criterion He places on that is we worship Him in
spirit and in truth (John 4:23-24). The Word tells us that God is a
God of love, mercy, and grace. When we read Lamentations 3:22
the prophet Jeremiah tells us that it is because of the Lord's mercy
we are not consumed. He is a faithful God (Deuteronomy 7:9). God
is always going before us protecting us from dangers we never even
knew existed.

When we change how we think about God and begin to see Him
as a loving Father Who only desires our sincere love in return, then
we will channel that love toward Him in worship. I challenge you

to re-examine your personal view of God. May you then experience a new freedom to worship you have never known before.

The Hope We Have in Our Praise

Bless the Lord, O my soul! O Lord my God, Thou art very
great; He makes the clouds His chariot; He walks upon
the wings of the wind;
(Psalm 104: 1, 3) (NASB)

I could have called this one "The Hope We Can Have. . ." But I
purposely chose to leave out the words "we can" here because
saying "we can have" raises the whether or not questions. Saying
what we "can" have raises doubt in our minds sometimes and might
leave the door open to the possibility that I "can't" have it. But
when I say what I **already have**, then there is no room for doubt,
questions, unbelief, or impossibility. What I'm getting at is this:
as believers in Jesus Christ we live in expectation of His return; as
Christians we live in hope everyday because of what Jesus did for us
at the cross of Calvary. We have hope because of Him.

When we praise God at a time when things are not going well,
we do so in hope. Two words that should never show up in the same
sentence are "Christian" and "hopeless." As believers we hope in His
grace; we hope in His return; we hope in His promise of everlasting
life; we hope in His favor; and we hope in the power of His Holy
Spirit.

Perhaps you are facing what is a painful situation, and it *appears*
hopeless. But I encourage you to turn your eyes to the God who rides
on the clouds, and walks on the wind. Let today's passage minister
to your spirit. You're not praising hope, you're praising the God who
gives us hope! May you begin again in hope and allow that hope to
take you through each day as God takes you to new levels in Him.

Worship: The Call From The Other Side

> . . .a great multitude. . .of all nations, and kindreds,
> and people, and tongues stood before the throne. . .
> And all the angels stood round about the throne. . .
> and fell before the throne on their faces, and worshiped God.
> (Rev. 7:9, 11) (KJV)

Worship is dangerous. There - I said it. It's out there. Why would I say that? Well, there are lots of reasons, but the most important one is worship brings exposure. Real, heartfelt, unabashed worship of God, be it public or private, is like opening the curtains in a dark house on a sunny day; light has now come into the house. Things are brighter, the darkness goes away, and new life comes into the house. In today's passage John is showing us a very vivid picture of the heavenly worship experience around the throne of God as seen through his eyes.

John's picture of what is happening includes people from every nation and tongue before the throne worshiping God. They were not quiet about it, either. Verse 10 of this chapter says, "with a loud voice" they blessed God! Please hear me. We are living in the last of the last days, and we have been for some time now. God is calling us to a higher place - the place of worship! The place of exposure. There is pain and confusion everywhere we look; all kinds of pain - inward and outward. We have got to stop just showing up at church; there is no danger in that. The danger is in your worship. In times of surrendered worship, whether public or private, we allow God to search our innermost being. We give Him free reign to make the necessary changes in our character so that we can go higher in Him. Sometimes when God is showing us our true selves it is not pretty, but it has to happen in order for us to grow and move from where we currently are to the place He has ordained for us.

Churches all over the country have a "Call to Worship" listed in the bulletin every Sunday, and I'm not knocking that. But the challenge is to move that Call off the paper and into your heart, and from there an outflow that answers the Call in your daily life. The Call really isn't from this side, but the other.

Worship: Not Where, But How

Our fathers worshiped in this mountain, and you people
say that in Jerusalem is the place where men ought to
worship. But an hour is coming, and now is, when the
true worshipers will worship the Father in spirit and truth;
for such people the Father seeks to be His worshipers.
(John 4:20, 23) (NASB)

When I really took a close look at the who, when, where, why,
and how questions surrounding praise & worship, I found it
interesting that the Word of God answers all of those questions on
the praise side, but not on the worship side. Thus far in my Christian
experience I have only found the who, how, and why questions
answered when it comes to the worship of God. We worship Him in
spirit and in truth because, according to scripture, that is what He
wants. In today's passage the Samaritan woman at the well was more
concerned about geography (where worship was to take place). That
was not the issue then, and it is not now. We know that in heaven
the praises and the worship of God are ongoing in the literal, eternal
presence of a Holy God. Here on earth we can pick our times of
worship, both public and private.

But worship has never been about the *place* because many gather
at the *place* of worship, but do not worship. Some may praise for a
minute, but their praise does not travel with them when they leave.
So what is the point here? The point is that God has given us just
one criterion and one reason for worship: He wants us to worship
Him in spirit and in truth - Holy Spirit-led worship, and according
to the truth of scripture. His concern is not with a building, or tent,
or any other man-made fixture or location. Both praise and worship

begin in a sincere heart that seeks to stay connected to Him. He's not even concerned with what day of the week it is. He is worthy of our worship every day.

When your heart is sincere toward Him you can worship wherever you are because you understand it isn't about location; it is about obedience to His one how-to in worship: "in spirit and in truth."

Praise God for HIS Plans

For I know the plans I have for you, declares the
Lord, plans to prosper you and not to harm you,
plans to give you hope and a future.
(Jeremiah 29:11) (NIV)

When the Holy Spirit unpacked today's passage for me I had to shout! One thing He told me was that God always knows the what and when of our lives. It's not that God doesn't care about our plans; He just wants us to line our plans up with His plans. He wants us to seek Him before we make plans. The number one point the Holy Spirit wanted to drive home for me is the fact that God DOES have a plan for our lives! We don't have to wander about in life lost with no direction. God's Word is crystal clear in that he has a plan, and He goes on to tell us what a piece of the plan is: He wants to prosper us, give us hope, and give us a future. You may not understand what is happening in your life right now, but I encourage you to meditate on this passage. God knows His plans for our lives. He just lovingly waits for us to line up with Him. No, we may not understand His plans the way we would like, but that's okay. The words "prosper," "future," and "hope" are enough to make my spirit jump; first because scripture backs them, and second because it just lets me know God is in complete control. Nothing just *occurs* to God. He is not a God of happenstance; He is a God of providence.

You may not see the plan based upon whatever it is you may be experiencing in your life right now. But please know this: God has a future and a hope for you. If you dwell on these truths in His Word, God will reward you greatly. He'll give you so much peace you won't be able to stand it. Relax, steady yourself, and allow His Word to minister to your spirit.

Keep Headquarters Close

Draw nigh to God, and he will draw nigh to you.
Cleanse your hands, ye sinners, and purify
your hearts, ye double-minded.
(James 4:8) (KJV)

When we hear the term "headquarters" what normally comes to mind is the "meeting place," or "the place where everything is going on," or even "starting place." Or we can even say the term "headquarters" denotes the place where needs can be met or perhaps protection can be found. Certainly at headquarters instructions can be given before proceeding further. It is a place of authority. If in this particular juncture in your Christian walk you feel lost, or in the dark, or can't quite find your direction, I challenge you to worship God. I believe that worship is an avenue, along with prayer, that will get us to Headquarters. The throne of God is the meeting place or the place of authority when we find ourselves in need of instruction before we move forward.

When military officers are reassigned to another unit, they must first check in with the commanding officer at headquarters to receive final instructions. When attending a convention there is usually a hotel, or convention hall that serves as headquarters where everything actually begins and instructions are received. Learning to worship God on a daily basis, and making regular study of His Word a priority will ensure that we keep headquarters in sight. When a military soldier has been reassigned, usually the commanding officer at his new post has already been informed of his coming. Each knows something about the other. God knows everything there is to know about us; how much in relation to your current need or desire do you know about Him?

Praise in Christ

There is therefore now no condemnation to them which
are in Christ Jesus, who walk not after the flesh, but after
the Spirit. For the law of the Spirit of life in Christ Jesus
hath made me free from the law of sin and death.
(Roman 8:1-2) (KJV)

I have often written that many people have the improper motivation
for praising God. Some praise the song, others praise the worship
leader, and still others praise the preacher. But this was never God's
intention. God's purpose in praise has always been grounded in
Himself. He has issued warning to us in scripture that He is a
jealous God and will have no other gods before Him (Exodus 20).
There is so much in today's passage, but I wanted to share with you
a wonderful confirmation and incredible blessing I received in a
recent Wednesday night Bible study. The Pastor was talking about
being in Christ, and I saw praise very clearly in that. There are people
who sit *in church* every Sunday, but they are not *in Christ*. Therefore,
their praise is not properly aligned, and consequently, they miss the
presence of God in worship. It does not have to be that way.

When we recognize as Christians who we are because of Jesus'
death, burial, and resurrection it should cause us to grow closer to
Him. It should make us want to know more about this Jesus who has
made us free when we received Him as Savior. The knowledge that we
are in Christ should revolutionize our praise and worship experience.
It should positively affect every area of our lives. Knowing we are in
Christ ought to redirect our thinking, our actions, our prayers, and
the goals we set for ourselves.

I have made a new commitment to more fully realize who I am, not in myself, but in Christ. I pray you make the same commitment.

A "Yea, Though" Praise

Yea, though I walk through the valley of the shadow of
death, I will fear no evil: for thou art with me. . .
(Psalm 23:4) (KJV)

For those of us who grew up in church, the twenty-third Psalm
is one of the first passages of scripture that we learned as very
small children. I cannot speak for anyone but myself here, but as a
child all the twenty-third Psalm was to me was a recitation when
called upon, or perhaps a blessing over a meal. As I got older, and
as I matured both as a person and as a Christian I began to see this
scripture in a new light. As I began to embark on a more meaningful
Christian experience, and go through some storms and uncertain
times, this particular psalm began to take on new meaning. I came
to understand that even when I'm going through a difficult period
God is going through it right with me. The passage says not only am
I in the valley, which is bad enough, but I am in the very shadow of
death. But the good news is God is with me. The other good news
is that I am walking *through* the valley - not taking up residence
there!!

We all know David was a praiser. God referred to David as a man
after His own heart. David praised God so intently and so intensely
when the Ark of the Covenant was brought back to Jerusalem that
he literally danced out of his royal regalia. But he wasn't dancing to
be seen of men; He was dancing before the Lord.

I do not know what you are going through today, but I want to
encourage you to keep a "yea, though" praise! Say to yourself, "Yea,
though, I'm in the valley; yea, though I have more bills than money;
yea, though I'm unemployed; yea, though no one but God seems to

understand my struggles, I still know God is **with** me. He hasn't left me alone. For Him to leave me alone would go directly against His Word. Yea, though the American economy has gone mad, I choose to live not according to the world's economy, but God's. God is not a man that He should lie, neither the Son of Man that He should repent. What He said in His Word **will** come to pass." I hope today you will choose to have a "yea, though" praise!

Power, Pressure, and Praise

But ye shall receive power, after that the Holy Ghost is
come upon you; and ye shall be witnesses unto me both in
Jerusalem, and in all Judea, and in Samaria, and unto the
uttermost part of the earth.
(Acts 1:8) (KJV)

Behold, I give unto you power to tread on serpents
and scorpions, and over all the power of the enemy:
and nothing shall by any means hurt you.
(Luke 10:19) (KJV)

I suppose it would be an easy thing to praise God for His power
in our lives. But what happens when it seems the power has
departed? What if there was a moment or even an extended season
when you did not feel God's power in your life? There is a myriad
of reasons we may feel this way - some self-imposed, and some not.
But what if all you feel day in and day out is pressure? Pressure from
all sides - work, home, finances, relationships, your dreams don't
appear as clear as they used to, your goals seem far away, and we
could go on and on. You feel all this pressure building on the inside
of you, yet your spirit is strong because you have too much Word
on the inside of you to bow to all the pressure. Deep in your spirit
you remembered David saying in Psalm 34:1 "I will bless the Lord
at all times. . ." Then perhaps you made a decision, like the psalmist
in Psalm 104, verse 33 to ". . .sing praise to my God while I have
my being." Maybe you have been like Jeremiah; the prophet was
under such pressure he didn't want to speak anymore for God, but
the Holy Spirit's fire burned within him to such a point he found

he couldn't quit - He could not release himself from the assignment God had given Him.

Somebody reading this right now knows God has given you an assignment, and you have tried to dismiss yourself from it, but you know God has not released you. You have just enough Word down on the inside to keep moving forward. God is always giving you a reason to forge ahead in spite of the pressure you face. There will always be pressure on some level from various sources. However, God has given us power, and he has given us weapons. One of those weapons is unending praise. No, you don't always feel like praising God, but the thing about God is He has not called us to act on our feelings; He has called us to act on His Word. His Word commands praise - He places no provisos on our current mood or circumstances. He wants our praise and our worship. Push through the pressure with your praise.

I Walk with God

I am the vine, you are the branches; he who abides in Me
and I in him, he bears much fruit; for apart from Me you
can do nothing.
(John 15:5) (NASB)

Some years ago, Rev. James Cleveland performed a powerful song
called "I Walk With God." A portion of the lyrics went this way:
"If you take Jesus as your partner, He will make your path much
brighter; and the key to my success is that I walk with God." I have
always liked this song, but at this stage of my Christian experience,
I can relate so well to it.

We can go all day naming Biblical characters who walked with
God. Jeremiah could not have felt that "fire shut up in my bones"
had he not made a life walking with God. The prophet Ezekiel
could never have obeyed God and preached to a valley of dry bones
if he had not made walking with God a priority. David had no basis
really to "bless the Lord at all times" if he lived his life far from God.
Abraham went looking for a city on God's instruction because he
walked close to God. Jesus walked close to His Father even unto
death on a cross.

God gives us so many reasons on a daily basis to bless His name.
As we study and live according to His Word, He is always giving
us a new reason to praise and worship Him. The fact that we have
breath in our bodies, strength in our limbs, and a mind to make
right decisions are testimonies of God's gifts to us. My prayer for
somebody reading this devotional is that you be encouraged to keep
walking with the Lord. Allow Him to train you for your future. I
love the Lord for that. I love Him because He can see down the road

so much further than we can, and He would not send us anywhere unprepared. We may feel unprepared and untrained, but God in His wisdom sees things much differently. Sometimes the training is painful when God has impregnated you with a vision and you are powerless to squelch it. Don't scoff at your suffering on your way to the manifestation of your vision. Keep walking with Him. Keep your mind on Him. Keep your vision ever in front of you. The best way to keep your mind on Him is to spend time with Him just worshiping. You can worship your way to a higher perspective. Continual praise will keep your mind on Him, too, but worship will usher you to a higher, much clearer perspective. You are going to see things differently when you lay on your face before God and just worship Him.

When you walk with God, you won't stay the same. You can't walk with God and stay in the same place. God is always calling us to a new level of praise, worship, prayer, and commitment. I pray that today you make the commitment to keep walking with God.

The Command in Service: Bless the Lord!

Bless the Lord, all you His hosts, You who serve Him,
doing His will. Bless the Lord, all you works of His, In all
places of His dominion; Bless the Lord, O my soul!
(Psalm 103:21-22) (NASB)

I have often said there are really only two places we can safely praise God: anywhere and everywhere. That pretty much covers it. David tells us to bless the Lord at all times and to always keep a praise in our mouths. Today's meditation, I believe, encourages those in Christian ministry in whatever area you may serve. This passage not only speaks to those in ministry, but to "all you works of His." "All places of His dominion" extends to every corner of the universe because God is the Creator of all.

If we are honest, even the most dedicated servants of God get tired. You love God with all of your heart and you are walking in your calling with a passion that only the Holy Spirit could have placed on the inside of you. There is physical and mental fatigue, but there is also a spiritual weariness from having labored, prayed, endured, and stood on the Word of God. However, we have seen no tangible change on heaven's part in our current situation.

In the years I have been involved in the ministries of praise and worship, what I have always found interesting about God is that He does not *request* we praise Him, but He commands it. He is not asking us to praise Him, He is telling us; and He is *adamant* about it. If you're reading this and you have grown tired in your service to God, just be still; don't speak, but let God speak to you. And if you do speak, be sure you only allow words to come from your mouth that edify. He knows your heart, now you listen for what is on His heart.

When I Say "Thank You," You Say, "Jesus"

O give thanks unto the Lord; call upon his name:. . .
(Psalm 105:1(a)) (KJV)

. . .for his name alone is excellent;
(Psalm 148:13(b)) (KJV)

When was the last time you were thankful to God? Have you ever been at the point where all you **could** say was "Thank you, Jesus"? Sometimes we say "thank you" and "Jesus" in the same sentence. Other times we just say "thank you" and God knows that in our hearts we are directing thanks toward Him. And yet there are other times we just say, "Jesus." It could be in prayer, or in response to a shocking situation. Perhaps the pain, confusion and disappointment in your own life is so abundant that all you can fix your mouth to say is "Jesus!" But whether you speak them together, or separately, either way is alright because the Word instructs us to give thanks. Even more importantly, we know from the psalmist that just His **name** is excellent. We know He does marvelous things; He is always doing that. But if He doesn't do another single thing for us, His **name** will still prove excellent!

We live in turbulent times. Some of the local or national news stories are so deplorable, so appalling that often all I can say is "Jesus!" Saying "thank you" is indicative of appreciation or gratitude. The name of Jesus, in all of its excellence is sometimes all we need to say because when we say "Jesus" we line up with the One who is eternal on His throne; the Lord of lords and the King of kings. When we say "Jesus" out of a sincere heart that is connected and attached to Him, it will bring peace to the troubled heart. So turn your "thank you" into a praise. When you say the name Jesus let Him usher you into a personal worship service.

A Praise Revival

But the Lord was with Joseph. . . and that which he did,
the Lord made it to prosper.
(Genesis 39:21, 23) (KJV)

And Joshua spoke to the house of Joseph, to Ephraim and
Manasseh, saying, "You are a numerous people and have
great power;. . .but the hill country shall be yours. For
though it is a forest, you shall clear it, and to its farthest
borders it shall be yours. . ."
(Joshua 17: 17, 18) (NASB)

I've just experienced a praise revival. No, I didn't attend a five-night church service and hear five sermons on praise. I'm talking about a renewing; a refreshing; a refinement; a re-directed focus. Perhaps it was a *praise resurrection* - yes, I think that phrase describes it well. Not that my praise was dead, it just needed to be pumped up a little. Have you ever experienced a period where you still had a praise, but it just needed a little push?

Today's passages just put a little more muscle to my praise. Even in Joseph's literal prison experience, the text says God was with him. And if you read a little further into Genesis you will see that God was with him so much so, that he named his second son Ephraim because "God has made me fruitful in the land of my affliction" (Gen 41:52).

I don't know what you are dealing with today, but I pray you will let these meditations minister to your spirit. God will never make His Word into a lie. Just as God was with Joseph, He will be with you. God was with Joseph, and Joseph was with God. As God caused Joseph to prosper He will cause you to prosper. We can lay hold on what Joshua told the tribes of Manasseh and Ephraim, in that we are a great people and have great power. Maybe all you see is trees - you know the hill country is yours because God gave it to you. Cut the trees down! Joshua told them in essence, "Yes, it's a forest, but it's your land; cut the trees down!" Do not doubt your God-given purpose, and do not doubt the power of our God. He is with you, and if you stay with Him you will prosper and possess what God has for you. What have you been waiting to do? What have you been afraid to start? In whose hand have you laid your future? Think about it.

Now Unto Him

Now unto him that is able to keep you from falling. . .
To the only wise God our Savior, be glory and majesty,
dominion and power, both now and ever. Amen.
(Jude 24(a)-25) (KJV)

Now unto him that is able to do exceeding abundantly
above all that we ask or think, according to the
power that worketh in us. Unto him be glory in
the church by Christ Jesus throughout all ages,
world without end. Amen.
(Eph. 3:20) (KJV)

With each new year comes new joys to experience, new challenges to conquer triumphantly, and fresh power to pass every test. But if you are someone who began the new year with dread, please consider today's meditations. These passages say that God is able. We can stop and shout right there! But there's more. They go much further to assure us what God is **able to do**. While one says He is able to keep us from falling, the other says He is able to do much more than we could ever ask or think. God is able to do things we have not even yet thought about. God's ways are so much higher than our ways; He is able to put things together in ways we could never have imagined.

When you have unanswered questions in your life, continue to make your praise *unto Him*. When you don't know what else to do; or when the words you want to say in prayer just will not come, keep offering your worship *unto Him*. When you offer praise and/ or worship unto Him out of a sincere heart, and as you continue to seek God with a spirit of expectancy, don't worry - He'll find you! Now. . .unto **Him**.

Let Judah Go Up First

Now the sons of Israel arose, went up to Bethel, and
inquired of God and said, "Who shall go up first
for us to battle against the sons of Benjamin?"
Then the Lord said, "Judah shall go up first."
(Judges 20:18) (NASB)

We know from Genesis chapter 29 that Leah named her 4th son Judah because with his birth, she chose to praise the Lord. Perhaps it had become evident to her that giving birth to three sons had not brought Jacob any closer to her in love. Therefore she made a conscious decision; she said, "this time I will praise the Lord"(Gen. 29:35 NASB). Leah turned her focus to God instead of naming yet another child out of Jacob's lack of love for her. It is from this passage that we derive the meaning of the term Judah, being "praise."

I want to challenge those of you who may be neck-deep in battle right now. In the heat of your spiritual battle let the praises of God go forth out of your mouth. Let the praises of God be as rivers of living water flowing from your belly (John 7:38). Before you spend hours just talking about the problem and how bad things are, stir up the power that God has already given you in your praises to Him; sacrificial though it may be. This is the kind of praise that reaches the heart of God. It is this kind of faith-building praise that will sustain you while you wait on God. This is the kind of praise that will keep you focused on God's promise, His plan, and His provision; it will keep you grounded in His faithfulness, and determined to press into your blessing.

Life continues to throw curve-ball challenges our way. We cannot escape them, but we don't have to fall prey to them. The lifestyle praiser recognizes that our responsibility is to apply today's passage to that situation you're facing. Don't open your mouth until you can say what God says. Don't say a word until you can formulate a praise, or a "Hallelujah!" on your lips! Praise will help you hold up until God shows up! Let *Judah* go out of your mouth FIRST.

Let Judah Go Up First, Part 2

Seven times a day I praise You, Because of Your righteous
ordinances.
(Psalm 119:164) (NASB)

When they began singing and praising, the Lord set
ambushes against the sons of Ammon, Moab and Mount
Seir, who had come against Judah. . .
(2 Chronicles 20:22) (NASB)

At times many of us reflect on things that did or did not happen, plans that were or were not quite fulfilled, things we wish we had or had not done, and the like. But think of it this way: God was in control of all of it. Even though we laid our plans well, or so we thought, God was still in control. I have learned many lessons over the years, but I feel the most important was that I should make plans loosely. What I mean by that is it's okay to make plans, but make plans in light of God's will for our lives; make plans with the full understanding that God, in His wisdom, can change them. He can do that - He's God. And don't always expect Him to discuss with you His changes. I've been there, believe me! The Word of God says that God's ways are above our ways (Isaiah 55:8-9).

I want to encourage somebody to start now giving over to God the coming days. Start now to commit your future to God; whether the next day or the next year! Pour out your heart to God now! Praise Him for what He brought you through. Praise Him for what He gave you, and for what He **didn't** give you. Praise God for the changes you had to encounter that you didn't see coming. Praise Him sacrificially for those life situations that you didn't ask for, could not control, and certainly could not stop. Give Him some praise because He *kept you* through it. He saw to it you didn't lose your mind. While you were crying because you didn't understand, God was keeping you. When you were desperate for answers, God was holding you.

In the Hebrew, the term "Judah" refers to praise. I want to challenge all of us to let Judah go before you into your future. Start a new day or a new year praising God, go through each day praising Him, and finish the day praising Him. And not just once on Sunday; choose to make praise to God intentional every day. When you go through your trials and tests learn to praise God in the very midst of them. Difficult? Yes, sometimes. Empowering? Always!

Some Reasons to Praise God

> He gives wisdom to wise men, And knowledge to
> men of understanding. It is He who reveals the
> profound and hidden things; He knows what is in
> the darkness, And the light dwells with Him.
> (Daniel 2:21(c)-22) (NASB)

We live in a world where some believers need a reason to praise God. In other words their relationship with God is perhaps not yet at the level where they keep a praise ringing in their hearts for no particular reason at all. Some of us just live in the reality that God is ever worthy of our praises and so we do not wait for the miraculous or the profound; we offer God praise because He's just that kind of God.

But for those who need a reason, then I invite you to consider today's text. Daniel was in a situation where his life was literally on the line. He inquired of God for wisdom to respond to King Nebuchadnezzar concerning a dream he had. Have you ever wanted an answer from God right now? You felt you had prayed and waited long enough, and it was time for God to bust a move. The text says that wisdom and power belong to God. It goes on to say that God reveals the profound and hidden things. He knows what is in the darkness. Now those are some mighty good reasons to praise God! Praise Him for His wisdom, His power, and how He will show it all to us when we ask Him. Now that's shouting news to me because what is in the dark will not remain in the dark when we walk with the One who holds light.

After God revealed Himself to Daniel, and equipped him to go back to the king with an answer, he praised God. I hope you are one of those people who can just praise God at the drop of a hat. But if not, my prayer is that you will consider these to be good, solid reasons to praise given to us by this prophet of God.

Some Reasons to Praise God, Part 2

> Then the mystery was revealed to Daniel in a night
> vision. Then Daniel blessed the God of heaven; To Thee,
> O God of my fathers, I give thanks and praise, For
> Thou hast given me wisdom and power; Even now Thou
> hast made known to me what we requested of Thee,
> For Thou hast made known to us the king's matter.
> (Daniel 2:19, 23) (NASB)

In Part 2 of our Reasons to Praise series, Daniel is praising God because God had revealed to him the mystery of King Nebachadnezzar's dream. This dream was troubling to the king to such an extent that he sent for the wise men of Babylon to interpret, but they could not. In his anger, the king issued a death warrant to all of the wise men of that region. At this point Daniel did a bold thing. He asked the king to give him some time to interpret his dream. Daniel then got his three friends involved; Hananiah, Mishael and Azariah, and they prayed to God for mercy. When God revealed Himself concerning the king's dream, Daniel went into a private praise service. He began to thank and praise God for showing His wisdom and power.

Revelation is a good reason to praise God. Revelation will send you into God's presence, and God's presence will bring revelation.

Then Daniel did another bold thing: he went to the man appointed by the king to destroy the wise men of Babylon, and in essence, said to him, "Don't destroy the wise men! Take me to the king and I'll tell him what he wants to know."

Today, if you need a reason to praise God, I'll give you two: praise Him for revealing your mysteries, and for giving you boldness when you need it that can only come from Him.

Some Reasons to Praise God, Part 3

> Since therefore, brethren, we have confidence to enter
> the holy place by the blood of Jesus, let us draw near
> with a sincere heart in full assurance of faith, having
> our hearts sprinkled clean from an evil conscience
> and our bodies washed with pure water.
> (Hebrews 10:19, 22) (NASB)

One of the reasons church folk don't worship when they get to church is because they are afraid. Coupled with not understanding true worship, it scares them because they know God well enough to know that if they really surrendered themselves in worship, God would reveal some things to them. So they think in order to keep themselves from being accountable to God, they just don't put themselves in any position to hear from God. And when they do hear, they don't yield.

But Jesus has fixed it so that we need not fear entering into His most holy presence. Today's text tells us that we have *confidence* to enter the holy place by the blood of Jesus!! That is a mighty, mighty good reason to praise God. When Jesus died on the cross the veil of the temple was rent from top to bottom, meaning it was literally torn. What this meant to the believer and the unbeliever who chooses to follow Jesus, is that no barrier exists to enter God's holy presence. In Biblical days only the high priest could come into the most holy place, and then, only once per year; to atone for his own sins and those of the people. There was a veil of separation in the tabernacle. But Jesus' death, burial and resurrection eliminated that. We don't have to wait for the preacher to get us to Jesus because at the cross, the veil was torn giving every believer direct access into His holy presence.

If you have accepted Jesus as your Savior, and He is Lord of your life, but you still have a hard time worshiping Him, just plead the blood of Jesus! If you have a relationship with the Lord, but you feel like you've messed up so bad you can't go to Jesus, just begin to plead the blood. The Word of God says we have access through Jesus' shed blood. You can praise God for the blood!!

Some Reasons to Praise God, Part 4; The Prophecy, Provision, and Purpose

I, even I, am the Lord; And there is no savior besides Me.
(Isaiah 43:11) (NASB)

Remember ye not the former things, neither consider the
things of old. Behold, I will do a new thing: now it shall
spring forth; shall ye not know it? I will even make a way
in the wilderness and rivers in the desert. This people have
I formed for myself; they shall shew forth my praise.
(Isaiah 43:18-12, 21) (KJV)

The 43rd chapter of Isaiah is so powerful. All through the chapter God is making Himself known; He is letting us know Who He is. There is so much in this chapter, but I want to help somebody today recognize that God has something *new* for you! He is admonishing us to forget what was, and have a mind toward what is to come! God is telling us to not even think about the past. Don't meditate on what was. Not only is He telling us He will do a new thing (the prophecy/promise), but He says He will even let us see it. He makes a similar proclamation in Isaiah 42:9. God loves us so much that not only will He make the promise, but He will show it to us. We can rejoice because God is a man of His Word. He is watching over His Word to perform it (Jeremiah 1:12)!

But then there is the provision in verse 19. God says He will make a roadway in the wilderness and supply water in the desert. Only God can put water where there is not normally supposed to be water. He is a supernatural God. If you feel right now you are walking through a wilderness experience, or the streams in your life have run dry, I encourage you to ponder Isaiah 43.

The purpose in all of this is found in verse 21. God says, in essence, "My people will declare My praise." In other words, He will get the glory in all of this. It is not for us to praise our own efforts, but it is all for **His** praise. It is to the praise of **His** glory. I've been there. I have had to push through by faith alone. I couldn't see anything but Him. But that is exactly where God wanted me. If I am describing where you are right now, be encouraged, and allow God to teach you to trust Him. Meditate on these verses; plant them deep in your spirit. God is taking you somewhere so wonderful you never could have formed it on your own.

Some Reasons to Praise God, Part 5;
Mercy by Day, A Song at Night

Why art thou cast down, O my soul?. . .hope thou
in God. . .the help of my countenance. Yet the Lord
will command his lovingkindness in the daytime, and
in the night his song shall be with me. . .
I will say unto God my rock, Why hast thou forgotten me?. . .
(Psalm 42:5, 8, 9) (KJV)

Have you ever felt like God had forgotten you? I have. In the deepest recesses of my being I knew He had not, but I felt like He had. Have you ever hurt so badly on the inside that nothing around you seemed to make any sense? And to make matters worse, God was silent. I can relate to how the psalmist felt when asked, "Where is thy God?" There are several rich nuggets in this psalm, but the one I want to focus on is found in verse 8. It tells us that God will command mercy in the daytime, and give us a song at night.

The psalmist says the Lord will command His lovingkindness in the day. That means there is no question; it is going to happen, and there's no stopping it. That is good news for somebody who is hurting right now because it says God has us on His heart during the day *and* at night.

One of the advantages of being called to the ministry of gospel music is that there is a song running through your mind at all times. My readers involved in music ministry know what I'm talking about. Perhaps those called to the preaching ministry say the same thing about sermon ideas. But there is no proviso or qualification here on who you have to be, or what position you hold. I believe any of us who have suffered over anything can relate to this one. We know the psalmist has cried quite a bit, is feeling down, and from all indications he sounds depressed. But even in his down-trodden state he finds in God hope, help, mercy, and a song. He still found a reason to praise God in spite of how he felt. God has a reason for everything He does, and He has a reason for giving us a song at night. Perhaps a night song and sleep are connected. Our Creator God knows every inch of our being; He knows that sleep is necessary for a healthy body and a clear-thinking mind. I want to suggest that the song in the night is conducive to peaceful sleep. Perhaps God had physical and mental rest in mind here. The message of a song will keep you going when you feel like giving up. It can settle your spirit and put your mind and heart at ease.

Be encouraged, as the psalmist was. If hope is all you have, then be certain that your hope is in God. Be assured that He will cover you with His mercy during the day, and fill you with a song at night.

One More Reason to Praise God: He Goes Ahead of You

And the Lord is the one who goes ahead of you; He will be with you.He will not fail you or forsake you. Do not fear, or be dismayed.
(Deuteronomy 31:8) (NASB)

The only thing we can be truly certain of in life on earth is that life is uncertain. This is true in every arena of life - home, work, our relationships with others, church life, competitors in business, school, etc. We make plans that may or may not succeed, no matter how well thought out. We work to make an acceptable grade in a class, and learn that our efforts were not as solid as we originally had hoped. You put all that hard work in your business and things didn't go as planned. What do you do when you really don't know what to do? What do you say in prayer when the words won't come? When you can't say or do anything else, speaking God's Word is *always* in order.

Moses was encouraging Joshua in this passage to finish the work that Moses started. Moses was old now, and unable to go forward. And further, God had already informed him that he would not cross the Jordan. It would now be Joshua's task to bring the children of Israel over the Jordan. When we chose to live a life of praise and worship to our God, we placed ourselves on the front line of a fierce spiritual battle. In other words, just as soldiers in a physical battle are often wounded, the same concept applies in the spiritual battle. There are darts, bullets, and scud missiles that fly all around us. The conflict is ever present; but for those who love the Lord and serve Him with a surrendered heart, we have help available. And for those who have not yet chosen to live for Him, that same help is available to you when you receive Him into your heart.

Isn't it wonderful to know that God goes before us? God is already in the not yet. We cannot see where He can see, except through the eyes of faith. We don't have the insight, the forethought, or the panoramic perspective that our God has. He is saving us from so much because He goes before us. He is preparing the way. We don't have to fear or be troubled because He said He would never fail us or forsake us. We are never alone. God said He would be with us! To me that is good news when I'm wondering what's going to happen next; when life's certain uncertainties seem to grip me so, that I want to give up. Then I remember that God has gone before me. He is preparing me, and He is preparing you, too. God has gone before you - move forward trusting Him.

Extravagant Worship, Extraordinary Praise

. . .and day and night they do not cease to say, Holy, Holy,
Holy is the Lord God, the Almighty. . .the twenty-four
elders will fall down before Him who sits on the throne. . .
and cast their crowns before the throne. . .
(Revelation 4:8,10) (NASB)

Your right hand, O, Lord, is majestic in power. . .shatters
the enemy. And in the greatness of Your excellence
You overthrow those who rise up against You;
(Exodus 15:6-7) (NASB)

This title may be problematic for some people because they cannot fathom the concept of extravagant worship; they have not yet grasped the worship part. The burden on my heart is that God's people understand that coming to church is not the same as worship. Only the intentional worshiper truly understands God is deserving of extravagant worship. In our reference text one group in heaven never stops saying, "Holy" while another group falls down before the throne and, as the text notes, they throw off their crowns and say, "Worthy." The Bible says this kind of behavior goes on all the time in heaven. Yet, here on earth, all many of us want to do is go to church on Sunday; we don't invite God to go with us, and don't invite Him into the service. If we do invite Him into the service, we stay His hand by not yielding to His presence; thus we limit His movement in the service and in our lives. After all that we leave Him at church following the benediction. God desires our continued fellowship with Him. If all of heaven can shower such great worship on Him, can we not do the same? Can we not offer up heart-felt, Spirit-led worship, whether in good times or bad?

Following their crossing of the Red Sea, and the total annihilation of Pharaoh's army, the children of Israel sang a song of praise to the Lord. They sang of His majesty, the Warrior He is, the greatness of His excellence, and how He works wonders. And if that wasn't enough, Miriam took her tambourine and went to work dancing before the Lord. Now I would certainly call that extraordinary praise! It wasn't half-hearted. It was all-the-way praise! David gave God an all-the-way, no-holds-barred praise when they brought the Ark of the Covenant back to Jerusalem.

I want to encourage somebody to let go and give God the worship and praise He so deserves. Maybe you've been so down this year that your faith has taken a beating and your praise has been, and perhaps still is, a sacrifice. I have good news - that's okay! Sacrificial praise is all the more pleasing to God. Go ahead and open your mouth and bless God's excellent name; go ahead and offer Him worship from deep inside you. When you do, you can experience the joy of the Lord come back into your spirit.

Encouraged To Praise

Now unto him that is able to keep you from falling, and
to present you faultless before the presence of his glory
with exceeding joy, To the only wise God our Savior, be
glory and majesty, dominion and power, both now and
ever. Amen.
(Jude 24-25) (KJV)

When was the last time you felt totally discouraged? You felt like giving up. Things were not going as you had so carefully planned, you prayed and nothing seemed to change, you praised, you worshiped, and you stood on the Word of God; all you had to hold on to was your faith, but you still felt discouraged. Today's passage was good news for me because I've been there. Many of you have been there too. Some of you reading this devotional are there; you may have been there for some time. But I want to encourage somebody.

We can unpack today's passage in so many ways because there is so much in there. But we can shout on the "able to keep you" part. No matter how much disappointment, rejection, and discouragement we may experience, God is still able to **keep** us. This may be a year of transition for you on many fronts, but guess what? God's promises never change. And His promise to us in today's scripture is that He is the only wise God, and power belongs to Him alone, no matter what our circumstance. My pastor, in a recent sermon spoke that we must make the promises of God bigger than our problems. And when we focus on His promises (and His Word is full of them), then our perspective changes in a most positive way.

God is not only our God, He is our Savior. He not only provides relief, but He provides salvation! Relief is temporary, but salvation is eternal! I can call up a friend or prayer partner and get *relief* to make me feel a little better, but only God provides salvation. We can quote a scripture or two and feel better about a thing, but when we have set our minds and hearts on the only wise God, meditate on Him day and night, spend time with him on a regular basis, and order our lives according to His plan and purpose, then we are candidates for salvation in our circumstances, not just relief.

God is a God of justice, and He will get justice for us when we place Him not second or third in our lives, but first! Please be encouraged, and don't be afraid to open your mouth with praise. You may not see your solution with the human eye, but as long as you can see God, you are certain to come out alright.

Worship: It Isn't Business - It's Personal

I am the Lord, that is My name; I will not give My glory
to another, Nor My praise to graven images.
(Isaiah 42:8) (NASB)

You shall have no other gods before Me.
(Deuteronomy 5:7) (NASB)

If I had to tag this devotional with a different title, it might be one concerning worship being our highest purpose in life. God has called us all to worship Him in spirit and in truth according to John 4:23-24. As a servant who has been charged with the responsibility of leading others into God's presence, I am constantly mindful of the fact that being at church every Sunday doesn't make the worshiper. Spending time with the Lord on a daily basis makes the worshiper. We must all remember that we are always in His presence, therefore, there is nothing God does not see. That is good news, especially for the chronic worshiper because as we spend regular time sitting at Jesus' feet, He comforts us in knowing He is very much aware of our pains as well as our joys.

In business settings, when a deal didn't go well, or someone lost his/her job, it has been said to the person who got the short end of the deal, "It's not personal, it's just business." And usually that statement isn't well-received, regardless of how well-meaning the messenger may have been. Well, that might work in corporate America, but not with God. You see worship is *very* personal to Him. He is not concerned with pomp and circumstance in our worship of Him. He is not impressed with grand displays, huge buildings, or congregations numbering in the thousands. His number one requirement for all creation is that our worship be led by His Spirit, and according to the truth of His Word. Is there a business side to ministry? Of course there is! But somewhere we have gotten it twisted and have allowed our worship to take on a different dimension than our Father intended.

When I first discovered that my service to the Lord had been tainted with business, I was attending a worship conference in Dallas. It was hearing Matt Redman's song, "Heart of Worship" that woke me up. All I had been bringing God was a song; I brought him my talent as a musician. That is not to say I was not sincere in my service, but worship was missing. God is not after great music, even though the Word of God speaks often of music. God is not after elaborate buildings, even though His own specifications for the building of the Tabernacle are very stringent and precise. But the order He laid out for the building of the Tabernacle was not about a piece of real estate, it was about His presence. God wanted a place that He might dwell among His people. And guess what? He still wants that. Whether on Sunday, or any other day of the week; whether sitting in church or at home, choose to lift your heart to Him in worship and experience that part of relationship that is so personal to Him.

Praising God Ahead of Schedule

But as for me, I will watch expectantly for the Lord; I will
wait for the God of my salvation. My God will hear me.
Do not rejoice over me, O my enemy. Though I fall I will
rise; Though I dwell in darkness, the Lord is a light for me.
(Micah 7:7-8) (NASB)

Sometimes, depending upon our individual maturity level in
Christ, when we are waiting for our prayers to be answered we
hold our praise until God actually manifests Himself. We schedule
our praise for when the blessing comes - when we can *see* it with the
physical eye. There are times we have to encourage ourselves in the
Lord, like David did. David was met with a pretty bad situation
the day he learned the Amalekites had raided Ziklag and taken
captive his wives, and those of his men. But the record says, "David
encouraged himself in the Lord his God" (I Samuel 30:6, KJV).
When you have prayed, acknowledged God, and gotten enough
of His Word on the inside of you, that qualifies you to praise God
ahead of schedule.

Most of the time as saints our schedule is never God's schedule.
He told us in His Word that His ways are higher than our ways.
But when you don't understand what's happening, constant and
continual praise will keep you strong during your test. I'm a witness.
Praising God ahead of schedule does not mean you are living in
denial; your problem is very real. But the difference is you have
chosen to dwell on the bigness of God through battering ram-type
praise and worship, rather than how big the problem seems. You
have made a decision to tell your problem about God, instead of the
opposite. It means you have so much Word in you that all you can

fix your mouth to say during your storm is, "Hallelujah, anyhow," even when you can't see the outcome.

When you praise God ahead of schedule you already know that God has put a super in your natural, so you have no problem giving God praise *before* you see your miracle, *before* you see that financial breakthrough, and *before* you get that job. Psalm 34:19 tells us that as Christians we will suffer many afflictions. We **all** face tests, trials, and challenges in our faith walk. But God's Word says He is a Deliverer. Maybe you have scheduled your praise for a certain time, but I want to challenge you to bump **your** schedule, and go ahead and praise God now because He loves us, gives new mercy every day, and fresh grace for every test.

Walk Toward Your Light

Thy word is a lamp unto my feet,
and a light unto my path.
(Psalm 119:105) (KJV)

Jesus said very clearly that in this world we would have tribulation. But He didn't stop there. He said, ". . .but be of good cheer, I have overcome the world" (John 16:33(b) KJV). Those verses in the Bible that have a "but" in the middle, I like to call *divine conjunctions* because it says to me that I should keep reading what is on the other side of that "but." That is where the blessing is going to be. Tribulation, or to put it another way, trouble, heartache, difficulty, affliction, confusion, brokenness, or a host of other descriptive terms, comes to all of us. It matters not our level of education or spiritual maturity. Regardless of how you define tribulation, it nevertheless points to a dark place in our lives - even for saints of God. There are times in all of our lives when God seems hard to find. Oh, He's there alright; we just, for a multiplicity of reasons, can't seem to put our hands on Him. But that is a good place to be.

When we don't know what to do, that positions us well for God to show His power and we will have had nothing to do with it. The Prophet Isaiah helps us here in Chapter 42 of his book. In verse 8 God tells us ". . .I will not give My glory to another. . ." Sometimes God places us in a position such that there is no way *we* can take the glory for what *He* has done.

Today's text says, God's Word is a lamp and a light. I have found out in my Christian experience that when I can't see my way, my next move is to walk toward the light of God's Word. Light will always pierce darkness. But the good news about God is that light and darkness are the same to Him, so He is not bothered by darkness. However, He is touched by our dark periods and He knows exactly where we are even if we do not! Don't ever think God doesn't see you. We may not always see Him, but He always sees us. Before He exchanged presence in the earth for eternal presence with the Lord, I often heard, a well-known Dallas pastor say, "Sometimes you have to trust God's heart when you can't trace His hand." That has stuck with me. When you can't see your way clear, and don't know what else to pray, that's alright. I have experienced those times. Just walk toward your light - the light of God's Word. If you stay in the light of God's Word, you will find an answer for every dilemma you face.

Repentance: A Neglected
Part of Our Worship

For I acknowledge my transgressions: and my sin is
ever before me. Against thee, thee only, have I sinned,
and done this evil in thy sight. . .Create in me a clean
heart, O God; and renew a right spirit within me.
(Psalm 51:3-4; 10) (KJV)

This will be the first in a series of devotionals dealing with seven
positions (or attitudes) that the true worshiper must take in order
for our worship to God to be effectual. The first position we will deal
with is repentance. When we come before God in worship, one of
the things we sometimes forget to do is repent. In our reference
scripture David is confessing and acknowledging before God his sin
of adultery, and that of having the husband of his partner in adultery
killed. Not only is David acknowledging what he has done, but he
says, "my sin is ever before me." David knew what he had done and
he wasn't blaming anyone else for it.

When we come before God in worship (not "coming to church;"
there is a difference) we must see to it that we bring a clean heart
before Him. The psalmist said only those who have clean hands
and a pure heart may stand in his holy place (Psalm 24:3-4). Just
about anybody can praise God, but not everyone can worship Him.
Worship is another matter entirely because it requires total surrender
on our part. It requires total focus on God and His worth, majesty,
and power. Worship requires a totally connected heart. Worship
requires an *attachment* to God, not just an *attraction* to Him.
Churches are filled every Sunday with people who are attracted to
Jesus, but never become attached to Him through salvation and

various available means of spiritual growth. The true worshiper not only understands what it means to worship God in spirit and in truth, but also understands that we cannot come to God any kind of way. True worship of God requires from us a pure heart and humility. When we come before a holy God in worship, He is not interested in our accomplishments, our status in the community, or how much money we put in the offering plate. He wants to know we are coming clean before Him, confessing our sins and choosing to live life His way. God just wants us to get real with Him.

Of all the things we lay before God in worship, let us remember to make repentance one of them.

Seek the Lord

Jehoshaphat was afraid and turned his attention to seek
the Lord, and proclaimed a fast throughout all Judah.
So Judah gathered together to seek help from the Lord;
they even came from all the cities of Judah to seek the
Lord.
(II Chronicles 20:3-4) (NASB)

Today's devotional is the second in a series dealing with the worshiper's position. The first position we dealt with was repentance. Today be encouraged to seek the Lord in your dilemma. We see from our text that king Jehoshaphat had received some dreaded news. Three armies were coming against him. He had just returned from battle when he gets word that another one is coming straight for him. The text tells us that after he acknowledged his fear, he "turned his attention to seek the Lord." But he did not seek the Lord alone. He gathered all of the cities of Judah together and proclaimed a fast all over the region. I like the fact that the king's prayer to the God of Israel began with worship! He did not begin by telling God what the problem was - that came later. He began by worshiping God and acknowledging His faithfulness shown to His people in the past. His prayer began with the confidence that God keeps His promises. Hallelujah!! Then God spoke through a Levite in the crowd named Jahaziel, giving them their instructions. After they heard God speak the first thing king Jehoshaphat and all of Judah did was worship! When God revealed Himself in that situation it drove them to worship. And after they worshiped, they obeyed, following God's instructions.

As you seek the Lord today, worship Him first, put Him in remembrance of His promises, and then position yourself to listen for His voice.

Be Strong and Courageous

> Be strong and courageous. . .Only be strong and very
> courageous; be careful to do according to all the law
> which Moses My servant commanded you; do not turn
> from it to the right or to the left, so that you may have
> success wherever you go. Have I not commanded you? Be
> strong and courageous! Do not tremble or be dismayed,
> for the Lord your God is with you wherever you go.
> (Joshua 1:6,7,9) (NASB)

There are instances in all of our lives that will eventually force us to dig deep within ourselves and call out an uncommon courage; perhaps a level we never thought we had because we never had to summon such courage before. Perhaps this was the case with Joshua. It certainly took courage to join Caleb with bringing back a good report, as opposed to the bad report of the remaining 10 spies who were sent to scout out the land of Canaan. Joshua and Caleb spoke before the entire Israelite nation that the land God promised was indeed good land, and they were well able to possess it. They saw the same land the other 10 spies saw, but their perspective was very different.

I believe that when God speaks the same thing more than once, He is trying to make a serious point. Four times in this chapter He tells Joshua to be strong and courageous. God already knew the courage it would take for Joshua to bring the children of Israel across the Jordan. He already knew the challenges Joshua and the Hebrew nation would face once they got across. Joshua had been trained and nurtured by courage. But now Moses has died, and it is up to Joshua to complete the journey into the Promised Land.

Sometimes it takes uncommon courage to worship, too. It takes much more courage to worship God than it does to come to church on Sunday. Getting to church is the easy part, even when we don't really feel like it. But the real challenge is getting into His presence in praise and worship once you get there. It takes courage to move yourself out of the way, and allow God to minister peace to your spirit. It takes courage to place the strange ways of the providence of God above your painful situation. When we live a life of praise and worship to God and surrender our total selves to Him in worship, we will recognize God's Jehovistic hand in every human circumstance.

How many of you know God has placed a dream in your heart? You have a very clear vision for how to make that dream a reality, but you lack the courage that will cause you to move forward. The Word of God says if we live life His way, and don't forget Him, He will make our way prosperous and be with us wherever we go.

The Worshiper's Position: Joy

". . .Do not be grieved, for the joy of the Lord is your
strength."
(Nehemiah 8:10(b)) (NASB)

For the kingdom of God is not meat and drink;
but righteousness, and peace, and joy in the
Holy Ghost. (Romans 14:17) (KJV)

There is a difference between happiness and joy - happiness is
dependent on things that *happen*. If great things happen we are
happy; if bad things happen, we're unhappy. However, the believer
can have joy regardless of what happens because while happiness is
wrapped in circumstances, joy, on the other hand is wrapped in how
closely we walk in the Holy Spirit. Our text makes it very plain. If
you read back a few verses prior to verse 10, you will see that Ezra
had been reading from the book of the law. As he blessed the Lord,
the people lifted up their hands and also bowed low to worship the
Lord. They had also been weeping while the book of the law was
being read, which brings us to verse 10. Nehemiah encourages them
not to be grieved because the joy of the Lord is their strength.

I see a whole lot in that verse. First, I have no reason to grieve
because my strength is in God. Second, it isn't *my* joy, but it is the
joy *of the Lord* that brings me strength. We can really dissect that
verse a number of ways: (1) the joy. . .is my strength, (2) the Lord is
my strength, and (3) it isn't my strength, and it isn't my joy.

Romans 14:17 is very clear in telling us where joy may be found.
The lifestyle worshiper understands this concept very well. When we
intentionally live our lives in praise and worship to God we line up
with eternity because God is eternal. We can be going through what

seems like hell, and still have joy. Adopting worship as a lifestyle does not provide us with an immunization shot against trouble, pain, or sadness. If you are one of those saints who has never experienced trouble in your faith walk, just keep on living. Life knows your address.

As worshipers we recognize that joy is the will of God. Regular church attendance alone will not secure your joy, but the Word says that walking close to the Holy Spirit will. As God reveals Himself to us in that process, we are driven to worship Him.

The Worshiper's Position: Total Trust

For thus the Lord God, the Holy One of Israel, has
said, "In repentance and rest you shall be saved,
In quietness and trust is your strength.". . .
(Isaiah 30:15) (NASB)

Worship should never be something we do only on Sunday morning. Why? Because Sunday is not the only day of the week God is worthy of our worship. And Sunday is not the only day we need to trust God. He is **worthy** every day, all day, no matter the season. No matter our station in life our worship to Him should be a lifestyle; a part of the very fabric of our being. Our reference scripture struck a chord with me because I had never thought of trust in terms of strength. But that is exactly what private and public worship does - it magnifies God to the point of taking the focus off of us, and placing it on the victories He has already won for us. This drives us to worship Him, which brings total trust on our part. I can testify that God will show Himself when we worship Him. Sometimes we forget what God has already done because we are so focused on the current problem.

Abraham was a worshiper. He trusted God so much that when God sent Him looking for a city, he went without question. Moses didn't become a worshiper until his burning bush experience, when God sent him to Pharaoh to get a job done for Him. Following Isaiah's worship experience in the year of King Uzziah's death, he trusted God enough to say, "Here am I, send me!" When king Jehoshaphat was faced with a battle he did not initiate, He basically told God, "We don't know what to do, but our eyes are on You."

Now that's trust! King Jehoshaphat made that statement **after** he had prayed, and **before** God spoke in the situation.

The challenge to all of us is to lift God so high in worship, until we experience that blessed quietness in our mind, body, and spirit. Worship Him until you arrive at that promise in Isaiah 26:3 that says "Thou wilt keep him in perfect peace, whose mind is stayed on thee: because he trusteth in thee." Notice God doesn't just promise peace, but **perfect** peace.

Stand in God's House

Behold, bless ye the Lord, all ye servants of the Lord,
which by night stand in the house of the Lord.
(Psalm 134:1) (KJV)

And the Levites of the children of the Kohathites, and
of the children of the Korahites, stood up to praise
the Lord God of Israel with a loud voice on high.
(II Chronicles 20:19) (KJV)

When it comes to standing or sitting during the praise and worship period in our church services, everybody still doesn't quite get it. If the President of the United States, a high-ranking government official, or other person worthy of such recognition were to enter the room, what would we do? Out of respect for this person's office we would stand. It would be shown as a matter of disrespect if we did not. If we can stand up for earthly authority, why not heavenly authority? God has been merciful and gracious enough to allow us another chance to walk into **His** house. If you are unable to literally stand up before Him, then your heart can surely stand in awe of Him. God will receive any heart that is completely yielded to Him. That is the proper order for all of us - heart, then body. But for those of us who are able to stand, what is our excuse? We serve a King; as a matter of fact, we serve THE King who deserves all of our reverence and respect.

In today's text, once God had spoken into their tense situation, we see that the king of Judah, Jehoshaphat, bowed his head with his face to the ground to worship, and all of Judah with him. Then the Levites stood up to praise the Lord with a loud voice. I like that -

they stood up! But they didn't just stand up without a purpose. They stood up to DO something! And they did it with a *loud* voice!

I challenge you today that when praise is going up in your church, stand up! When God is moving in the midst of worship **get up** and give Him all you have. Stand your body up, bring your heart to full attention, and acknowledge we serve a King who is able to accomplish all things for us (Psalm 57:2 NASB).

A Bowed Body

O come, let us worship and bow down: let us kneel before
the Lord our maker. For he is our God;. . .
(Psalm 95:6, 7(a)) (KJV)

And all the angels stood round about the throne, and
about the elders and the four beasts, and fell before
the throne on their faces, and worshiped God.
(Rev. 7:11) (KJV)

One of the most challenging, yet rewarding postures of worship I
have experienced is bowing low before God's presence. We serve
a God who is more worthy than our human imaginations could ever
fathom. Yes, He is worthy of our standing in His presence. However,
He is also pleased when we choose to bow low, kneel, or literally lay
flat on our faces before His presence. Lying prostrate before God is
probably one of the most humble bodily positions we can take. But
please remember that it matters not how low we bow if our hearts are
not involved. Our worship to almighty God will always be a matter
of the heart, regardless of what forms we may take.

In today's text we see the inhabitants of heaven bowing low to
worship the One who sits on the throne. If we say we love the Lord
and plan to spend eternity in heaven with Him, along with a host
of continual praisers and worshipers, then shouldn't we bow low in
worship while still on earth? We have plenty of human examples:
Jehoshaphat, king of Judah bowed low when he heard from God;
as Ezra blessed the Lord the people lifted up their hands and then
bowed low in worship; Solomon was kneeling when he prayed in
dedication of the newly-finished house of the Lord.

Perhaps it's going to take a level of desperation for some of us to bow low in worship to God. It takes **desperate prayer** to move to the next dimension in God. To take that a step further, it is going to take some **desperate worship** to get us there as well.

As we prepare for Christ's return, why not incorporate into your private worship, as well as the corporate worship experience times of bowing, kneeling, or going prostrate? In doing so we are positioning ourselves to hear from Him. Someone reading this devotional has been seeking God in prayer for a long time about something that only you and He know about. If you have never bowed low as you worship Him in prayer, I encourage you to bow your heart AND your body before Him and listen as He speaks.

Failure Is Not On The Agenda

And all these blessings shall come upon you and overtake
you, if you will obey the Lord your God. The Lord will
command the blessing upon you . . . in all that you put
your hand to . . .The Lord will open for you His good
storehouse, the heavens, to give rain to your land in
its season and to bless all the work of your hand . . .
(Deuteronomy 28:2, 8, 12) (NASB)

There are times perhaps in all of our lives when we felt we had
failed at something. And if you're like me, you beat up on
yourself because of it. Perhaps you said, "I didn't try hard enough,
didn't work hard enough, there must be something I didn't do right."
Sound familiar? Someone reading this might be feeling that way
right now. But God never created us for failure. Jesus came that
we might have life and have it more abundantly (John 10:10). Our
reference scripture for today states very clearly that when we walk in
obedience to God - when we walk *with* Him, and not *against* Him,
whatever we set our hand to do He will cause it to prosper. I am
not suggesting we won't suffer heartache or disappointment when
we obey God. But I am saying that we will be the better for having
obeyed Him in every area of our lives. Psalm 125:2 tells us that as the
mountains surround Jerusalem, so the Lord surrounds His people.
That's good news when the winds of failure attempt to blow into our
lives. God is surrounding us, He is holding us up, and has given us
the privilege of His mercy.

Let me say just a word about fear. The Bible says fear is a spirit
and it is not from God. It is destructive, and not only will it keep you
from walking in God's plan for your life, it will stifle your worship

of Him, whether public or private. There are people who fear failure, so they never attempt anything for God.

Please understand this: God is at perfect liberty to change our plans. He is sovereign and all wise. It really isn't about us. Our human resources are limited, but God never runs short of anything. Do what God has put in your heart. Right now decide for yourself, even by faith, that failure is NOT on your agenda. It is not on mine.

Dead Men Don't Argue

But I say, walk by the Spirit, and you will not carry
out the desire of the flesh. For the flesh sets its desire
against the Spirit, and the Spirit against the flesh;
for these are in opposition to one another. . .
(Galatians 5:16, 17) (NASB)

We often hear in our Christian experience about instances when we, or someone we know acted or spoke in the flesh rather than according to the Holy Spirit. In other words we acted or spoke in ways that pleased **us**, rather than pleased God. The Word tells us our human capabilities and our spirit man are constantly at war with one another. This is true in every area of our lives, and is no less true in our praise and worship to God. Many of us don't praise or worship God for varying reasons, but usually the culprit behind this rebellion is our flesh. God, speaking through the psalmist, has said in His Word, "Let everything that hath breath praise the Lord." The fleshly side of us won't allow it. We don't lift our hands in praise to the Lord because it is uncomfortable for us. We don't kneel at church out of concern for who is watching; we don't do it in private because we might feel kind of silly.

But when we have died to, or "crucified" our flesh, then we are more willing to give God Spirit-controlled, heart-inspired worship He so deserves. When our flesh is dead to pride and traditionalism we can give God the glory due His name. Our flesh wants to worship the way *we* want to worship. When we attempt to praise God through only our human faculties, we cannot employ the *at all times* kind of praise spoken of in Psalm 34:1.

Sometimes when life hurts the last thing our flesh wants to do is praise God. It is always difficult to praise God in the midst of our pain. But that is when we must command our flesh to move in the realm of the Holy Spirit. There are times when we have to literally **press in** to the courts of our God. God is pleased when we push past our feelings and religious traditions to operate in the power of the Holy Spirit. We give Him free reign to either change our circumstances, or change us in the midst of them.

When we are dead to our flesh we won't argue with God about praising Him according to His directive.

A Call To Pray

pray without ceasing;
(First Thessalonians 5:17) (KJV)

Today I just felt a need to pray. There are so many believers going through difficult times now - churches, preachers/pastors, families, work situations, finances, and the Body of Christ at large are under attack from the enemy like we have never seen. Believers and unbelievers alike are hurting on many different levels.

When you pray, worship God first. Acknowledge Him for Who He is and revere His name. Give Him the glory that is due His name. Pray for those who are hurting, whether the source is physical, emotional, or spiritual. Pray for those saints of God who, in the midst of discouragement have labored for the Kingdom believing God. Pray for those who have travailed in prayer, seeking God for release. Pray for those who have given God their all in ministry, yet have still suffered affliction. Even pray for those who don't know what it feels like to labor in prayer - don't know what it is to wait on God for an answer. They don't realize the power found in their personal worship of God. Pray for those who don't know what faith is because they have never had to call on Him in faith - everything has always been well with them - or so it seems. Pray that they recognize that it is God who has brought them where they are.

Pray for the Body of Christ, regardless of denomination. Pray that the Body would continue to stand on the truth found in the Word of God. Pray that believers everywhere would keep on believing. Pray that unbelievers would look around them and see what God is doing in the earth, and by the urging of the Holy Spirit begin to acknowledge Him. Pray that they would receive Him as

Savior. Pray for your co-workers and those who have the rule over you in the workplace. Pray that your light would continue to shine in the workplace, not only so that you can stand, but that God would direct you to those who need Him and share His love with them. Keep your light shining because a co-worker is watching you and headed your direction. He needs somebody to pray with him. Or maybe she just needs to talk to somebody.

Time is winding up. Don't wait to pray – do it now.

God Has Given Us Weapons: Are You Using Yours?

For the word of God [is] quick, and powerful, and sharper
than any two-edged sword, piercing even to the dividing
asunder of soul and spirit, and of the joints and marrow,
and [is] a discerner of the thoughts and intents of the heart.
(Hebrews 4:12) (KJV)

For the weapons of our warfare [are] not carnal, but
mighty through God to the pulling down of strong holds;
(II Corinthians 10:4) (KVJ)

A previous devotional, <u>Clean Your Gun</u> deals with using the praise of God as a weapon against the enemy. But the focus of today's devotional is on the Word of God as our main weapon. It is there that we learn how, when, where, and why we praise and worship God.

Our enemy, the devil, is working overtime like never before to destroy people, ministries, homes, relationships, churches, and anything else he can gain a foothold into. Our reference passage tells us very clearly how sharp and cutting God's Word is. Using God's Word against negative strongholds is one of the benefits we gained upon salvation through Jesus Christ. Salvation in the Greek is "soteria," which means safety, soundness, or protection. Following our salvation experience the next process that should begin is deliberate, continual growth in His Word, and intentional prayer. There was a television commercial at one time for one of the credit card companies that said, "Membership has its privileges." It meant if you held this company's credit card you could expect certain privileges and rights as a cardholder. Well, guess what? We have privileges and rights as members of the Body of Christ. Jesus gave us authority to use the Word in our lives; it is up to us to apply it. We have a right to expect God to honor His Word (Jeremiah 1:12; Isaiah 55:11).

But you cannot apply what you don't know. Pick up your Sword and begin reading it. Read it until you find peace; read it until you find release; read it until you find a solution to your problem. And then keep on reading until you find yourself meditating on it. I wasn't present at the drafting of the U. S. Constitution in 1776, but I have declared over my own life that The Word of God is *my* Bill of Rights; His Word is *my* Declaration of Independence over Satan's power attempting to operate in my life! And I know that as long as I practice the principles found in God's Word, I have power. Amen!!

What Are You Bringing to the Table?

Bless the Lord, O my soul; And all that is within me,
bless His holy name.
(Ps. 103:1) (NASB)

S adly, in many of our churches across the Body of Christ people sit in the pews, week after week, and miss worship. There are lots of reasons for this and that topic is far too broad to cover in a single devotional. However, I will share one of those reasons being some people don't bring anything with them to the worship experience - at least nothing of value to God. For example, a wounded spirit, a broken heart, a spirit of expectancy, or a praying and receptive attitude. We cannot just show up in service on Sunday morning thinking we're doing God a favor by being there. God wants more than that. He wants all of us - body, mind, and spirit. God doesn't just want your talents, he wants YOU. Everything concerning you, God wants to use it to glorify Him. He is, after all, our Creator and we find our being in Him. He is the ultimate Giver of life, and we owe Him everything. The time that we spend on Sunday morning, whether sitting in church or not, belongs to Him as well. God is under no obligation whatsoever to place breath in our bodies each day. He loves us so much that He chooses to let us breathe. So how **dare** we sit in church and act like we're all that?

Let us never think that simply because we brought our "bodies" to the church on Sunday morning that God is satisfied with that. He wants much more. Since God blesses us daily with extravagant grace, I believe we owe Him an extravagant praise, and a Holy Spirit-controlled worship encounter.

So I ask you: What are YOU bringing to the table?

Praise Him by Faith

Now the just shall live by faith. . .
(Hebrews 10:38) (KJV)

I will just cut to the chase on this one. Sometimes we have to praise God when everything around us dictates the contrary. Our outer environment may make it very difficult to give God a full praise; it happens every day. But oftentimes we must praise God by faith, and faith alone. We know that faith is believing something you cannot even see. So when we can't *see* any reason to praise God, we must train our spirit man to produce a praise anyway. God is concerned about those things we cannot see; otherwise He would not have said in His Word that He will perfect those things that concern us (Psalm 138:8). No matter your situation right now, stir up your faith and praise God in the midst of what you can't see. Not by might nor by power, *but by My Spirit*, saith the Lord of hosts (Zech. 4:6).

Don't Forget Your Benefits!

Bless the Lord, O my soul: and all that is within me, bless
his holy name. Bless the Lord, O my soul, and forget not
all his benefits:
(Psalm 103:1-2) (KJV)

When we accept a new job, there are certain benefits that come along with that job - paid vacation, medical insurance, life insurance for some, or perhaps a 401(k). And if you *really* have it like that a company car and expense account may come with the package. You didn't necessarily have to ask for those things; they just came with the job - "perks" if you will. The same is true in the spirit realm in our walk with the Lord. Walking with Him and blessing His name bring certain benefits. Today's reference passage lists many. He forgives all our iniquities, heals all our diseases, He redeems our lives from destruction, crowns us with lovingkindness and tender mercies, and on top of all that he satisfies our mouths with good things. He even renews our youth like the eagle's. As you move through this day, don't forget your benefits!

Praise Your Way Through The Darkness

> I will bless the Lord at all times: his praise shall
> continually be in my mouth. (Psalm 34:1) (KJV)

I write this as someone who understands fully how difficult it can be to bless the Lord at all times. It isn't always easy to bless the Lord when life has dealt us what appears to be a dirty blow. When pain, disappointment, and trouble comes our way through no fault of our own, it is hard to see any reason why we should bless Him at all times. But while all of these feelings are very real to us, God's Word is even more real. While the darkness seems very thick, remember the light of God's countenance can penetrate even your darkest moments. Start today to make what God has **said** be bigger and larger than what you can **see**. Magnify God and His Word rather than your problem.

Surrendered Worship

And he said, "No, rather I indeed come now as
captain of the host of the Lord." And Joshua fell on
his face to the earth, and bowed down, and said to
him, "What has my lord to say to his servant?"
(Joshua 5:14) (NASB)

One of the important aspects of worship is two-way communication.
Joshua had been trained and mentored by Moses; the man whom
the Bible says the Lord knew face to face (Deuteronomy 34:10). Prior to
his death, Moses had passed the mantle on to Joshua to lead Israel into
the Promised Land. Under Moses Joshua had been trained to serve God
and only God. He had been trained to worship God and obey Him.
So when this man standing before Joshua identified himself as captain
of the Lord's host, all Joshua knew to do was bow low and ask a very
pointed question: he said, in essence, "What do you have to say to me?"
I found today's passage interesting because not only did Joshua surrender
his heart and mind to hear, but he got his body involved also.

God is able to speak to us in whatever physical position we take,
but the first order of true worship is a totally surrendered heart and
will. Knowing this messenger had been sent by God, Joshua did
what was necessary to receive the word being delivered. There are
many instances in scripture where individuals or an entire nation
bowed low to worship God.

Worshipers understand surrender. For the true worshiper, there can
be no real worship without it. Today's challenge is to boldly surrender
everything to God - your heartache, your issues, your dreams, your joys
- literally everything and enter into a new level of worship. Then wait for
God to show Himself to you in a way you have never seen Him before.

Prayer and Worship: The Relationship

Pray without ceasing.
(I Thessalonians 5:17).

We know from scripture that there are two things God requires of us as Christians: prayer and worship. We have been instructed in God's Word to pray without ceasing. As any true prayer warrior will tell you, prayer is two-way communication between God and the person(s) praying.

Too often we deem prayer as only one-way communication when we talk to God but give Him no opportunity to talk back to us. We want what we want, but have not inquired of God what He wants. We make every effort to carry out our plans when in reality, we have not called in to Headquarters for the proper instructions. We told God our plans but did not wait for His answer. God has shown me in my Christian walk that He is at perfect liberty to change my plans, no matter how well-thought-out I had initially deemed them to be. When I went through an extended period of unemployment and the uncertainty in my mind was abundant, He let me know that my agenda meant little in light of His perfect plan for me. He taught me to humble myself all over again, and understand that it really isn't about my limited ability or resources, but His total sufficiency.

The same is true in our worship to God, be it public or private. When we enter into God's presence in worship, there should be two-way communication, as well. I believe that we can sometimes attempt to "manufacture" God's presence and His voice in worship. But we must understand that God is perfectly capable of speaking for Himself. Our job is as watchmen listening for His voice (Proverbs 8:34). We talk to God in worship – extolling Him for His greatness, wisdom, care, and love. And just as in our times of prayer, God desires to speak to us in our times of worship. Before I go any further, please understand that when I use the term "worship" I am not referring merely to church attendance. Regular church attendance does not make us worshipers any more than attending the opera makes us an opera singer. Having attended a church service begs two questions:

(1) Did you worship while you were there?
(2) Did you go to meet God or just be part of a gathering?

Prayer and Worship: The Relationship, Part 2

Not only does God desire sincere prayer, but He insists upon sincere worship as well. In Luke 18:11-13 as the Pharisee prayed thanking God he was not as other men, the tax-gatherer, aware of his own unworthiness pleaded to God for mercy. The prayer of the tax-gatherer caught Jesus' attention because he humbled himself. This was not so for the Pharisee. In Psalm 51 when David prayed for God to create in Him a clean heart, he states in verse 6, "Surely you desire truth in the inner parts. . .". The sole criterion God has given us for coming to Him in worship is "in spirit and in truth" (John 4:23-24). This kind of worship is Holy Spirit-led, and in a manner according to the truth of God's Word. As the children of Israel camped during their wilderness journey with the Tabernacle situated in the middle of the camp, so God Himself desires to be present today in the middle of our prayers and our worship. As Jesus taught the disciples to pray in Matthew 6:9-13, I found it interesting that The Lord's Prayer begins and ends with worship. It begins with "Our Father in heaven, hallowed be your name. . ." The word "hallow" points toward adoration or reverence. This prayer ends with "For thine is the kingdom, and the power, and the glory, forever, Amen." The kingdom is His, and the power and the glory are His also. Psalm 29:2 tells us to give unto the Lord the glory due His name.

There must be an inner devotion on our part toward prayer and worship. Both are matters of the heart. Our worship to God should be an outflow of what is already seeded in our hearts. That is when worship becomes a lifestyle as opposed to just a religious ritual performed only on Sunday morning. It is so much easier to talk to God in prayer when we have raised our prayer lives to the level of intentionality. After the Upper Room experience at Pentecost they devoted themselves to prayer, as well as fellowship and teaching (Acts 2:42).

Prayer and Worship: The Relationship, Conclusion

Another parallel we can draw between prayer and worship is our total submission to Christ's Lordship. When we go to God in times of need, we must come with the attitude that God owns everything. There is nothing we could ever ask God for that He does not already have. The silver and gold is His (Haggai 2:8). He owns the cattle on a thousand hills (Psalm 50:10). Psalm 24:1 tells us the earth is His, and all it contains. But the good news for those adopted into the family of God is that, because of the blood of Jesus, we are partakers of His very nature. What is His by *right,* is ours by *adoption,* and we have the privilege of receiving from Him when we ask in faith. The best move we can make when we need something from God is to begin to worship Him. To worship God in times of need says to Him, "I love You, You are still God, and I trust You. I have full faith and trust in Your sovereignty and Lordship in my situation." As we worship God in prayer it takes the focus off the need at hand, so that our focus shifts to God's power to meet the need.

One often-neglected aspect of prayer and worship is repentance. There are many instances in scripture where God invites us to tell Him what is on our hearts. But sometimes we are so concerned about telling God about our problem that we are not conscious of the fact that we need to repent. As Jesus teaches His disciples to pray, He admonishes them to seek forgiveness from God, and to practice forgiveness themselves. As David prays in Psalm 51 he acknowledges in verses 2-4 that he knows what he has done, and he doesn't blame anyone. He admits his sin before God. David was fully aware that he could not approach a holy God just any kind of way.

Both prayer and worship are faith ventures. It takes faith to seek God's face in prayer when we are tired of trying, and discouraged. It requires an absolute faith on our part to offer worship to God in times of uncertainty. Faith is believing something we cannot see. But intentional prayer and worship in the life of the believer sharpens our spiritual focus. It does not mean we will be immune from trouble or pain. It does mean, however, we can have peace in what can feel like the worst of times.

Neither prayer nor worship should be done for human approval. Jesus rebuked the Pharisees for offering such empty, self-indulgent prayers (Luke 18:11-12). God is not impressed with our eloquent language in prayer. All He wants is a sincere heart that desires to draw close to Him. So it is in our worship. Sometimes God just wants us to spend time at His feet. I can tell you that during times when I felt mentally, emotionally, and spiritually exhausted, God showed Himself faithful as I just sat at His feet to find rest. As I entered into times of worship, He spoke peace to my heart. I wasn't always sitting in church during these times of fellowship; sometimes I was alone at home, or in my car. I have even been at my job when the Holy Spirit rose up in my darkened state, and brought a divine light and settlement to my spirit.

I want to challenge someone today to include times of worship in your prayer life. Rather than always being in petition-mode, why not shift your prayer direction from petition to worship? As God honors the petitioner, so He honors the worshiper

The Best-Laid Plans

In every thing give thanks. . .
(I Thess. 5:18) (KJV)

Truth be known, we are all struggling with something. More often than we may care to admit we are thanking God in spite of. In spite of *what*, you might be asking? Well, you fill in the blank; only you can answer that question. The very familiar expression, "The best laid plans. . ." is usually followed by "sometimes don't work out." But God has His reasons when our well-laid plans, and what we believed were well-thought-out strategies just don't come to pass as we wanted. First, He is God. Second, His ways are higher than our ways. Third, He can see much further down the road than we can. Fourth, He loves us much too much to ever send us out unprepared. Fifth, even though we want something so badly God knows that there may be some things inside of us that He has to change; things that we can't take with us into that place He has for us. Hard pill to swallow? Yes. Is it a struggle? Absolutely. If you need a reason to be thankful, I just gave you five of them.

God's timing is always perfect. A friend had to help me with that one recently. My friend told me that if it happened according to my timetable and not God's, I would not be successful. I kept telling myself there has to be something I'm not doing right. But at the end of the day, God shows Himself in delay. He exposes some bad attitudes and wrong motives in times of delay. He gives us better ways of doing things when in delay. In case you missed it, delay is reason No. 6 to be thankful. I am learning to thank God for not giving me what I want when I want it. I still struggle with it, but He continues to show me love, grace, mercy, and wisdom. So stop asking the, "Everybody-else-gets-what-they-want-why-can't-I?" question, and try just being thankful.

Made in United States
Cleveland, OH
16 January 2025

13509585R00076